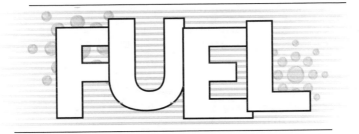

IGNITING YOUR LIFE WITH
PASSIONATE PRAYER

RANDY SOUTHERN

THOMAS NELSON PUBLISHERS®
Nashville

a division of Thomas Nelson, Inc.
www.thomasnelson.com

The publisher thanks The Livingstone Corporation for their assistance
with this title.

Published in Nashville, Tennessee, by Thomas Nelson, Inc.

Unless otherwise noted, Scripture quotations are from THE NEW KING
JAMES VERSION. Copyright © 1979, 1980, 1982, Thomas Nelson, Inc.,
Publishers.

Scriptures noted NCV are from *The Holy Bible, New Century Version,*
copyright © 1987, 1988, 1991 by Word Publishing, Nashville, Tennessee
37214. Used by permission.

Library of Congress Cataloging-in-Publication Data

Southern, Randy.
Fuel: igniting your life with passionate prayer / Randy Southern
     p. cm.
ISBN 0-7852-6748-4
1. Prayer. 2. Bible. O.T. Psalms—Criticism, interpretation, etc. I. Title.
BV210.2 .S635 2001
248.3'2—dc21   2001040336

Printed in the United States of America
01 02 03 04 05 PHX 5 4 3 2 1

For Amy & Brady,

Living Proof of the

Power of Prayer

CONTENTS

1   A Word to the Whys   1

2   Do You Know the One You're Talking To?   21

3   And How   41

4   Credit Where Credit's Due   59

5   Thank You, Thank You Very Much   79

6   Praying for Another   97

7   When I Find Myself in Times of Trouble   117

8   One to Grow On   137

9   Shhh, Listen!   157

10   Interference!   177

Acknowledgments   195

Other XT4J Stuff   197

1

A WORD TO THE WHYS

"Does that make your food taste better?"

David looked up and saw the guy at the next table staring at him. "Huh?" David asked, not sure whether the guy was talking to him or to himself.

"You were just praying, weren't you?" the guy asked.

"Yeah," David said slowly.

"I was just wondering if praying, like, makes your hamburger taste like filet mignon or something."

David took a bite of his burger, chewed it for a second, and said, "Nope, it's still a hamburger." Then he smiled at the guy and turned back toward his food, hoping that was the end of the conversation. It wasn't.

"Then why do you pray?"

Aw, come on, dude, David thought, just let me eat my food. He couldn't tell whether the guy was making fun of him or being serious, so finally he just said, "I was thanking God for my food."

"And you probably do that before all meals, don't you?"

"Yeah, I usually try to pray before I eat." David could hear the defensiveness creeping into his own voice.

The guy seemed pleased by David's answer. "Tell me this," he said as he leaned forward in his chair, "do you pray every time you get in your car or every time you deposit money in the bank?"

"No." David still couldn't tell where the conversation was heading.

"Why do you pray for some things and not for others?" the guy asked. "Aren't you thankful for your car and your money too?"

"Well, yeah, but—"

"Have you ever told God anything in prayer that He didn't already know?" the guy continued.

"What do you mean?" David asked.

"I mean, have you ever asked Him for anything He didn't already know you wanted?" the guy pressed. "Have you ever thanked Him for something that He didn't already know you were grateful for? Have you ever surprised Him with anything you said in one of your prayers?"

"Well, since God knows everything there is to know, I guess my answer is no," David admitted.

"Then why pray?" the guy repeated.

David looked down at his burger and fries, which were getting colder by the second. *I guess this is what I get for praying,* he sighed to himself.

it's like this

What if someone interrupted one of your prayers and asked, "Why are you doing that?" Would you have an answer?

(And, no, you can't count "Get out of my face" or "None of your business" as an answer.)

If you were to do a survey among the people you know who pray, you'd probably get at least a few reasons like these:

- "I pray when I'm in trouble."
- "I pray when there's something I really need."
- "I pray when I don't know where else to turn."

These can be legitimate reasons to pray, but they're not the only reasons to pray. And if extreme prayer is your goal, then you need to discover why God wants us to come to Him in prayer.

And the psalmists are just the guys to show you.

Open to any psalm in the Bible and you'll find a master-piece of prayer. God thought so much of the psalms that He included them in His Word. You can't get higher profile than that. These prayers were so meaningful that God wanted people to be able to read and learn from them thousands of years later.

These weren't quickie requests tossed off whenever the psalmists had a spare moment. Look at the language and com-position of a prayer like Psalm 119. The author of this psalm put some serious thought into what he wanted to say to God.

The Bible is crawling with such prayers—not just the 150 in the book of Psalms itself, but the dozens of others scat-tered throughout Scripture. It's obvious that a lot of work went into all of them.

And the question we need to answer is *why*. Why did the authors of the biblical psalms put so much effort into their prayers? What did they hope to gain? What did they want from God? What was their motivation? Let's take a closer look at why the psalmists prayed, drawing clues from their very prayers.

Word

Right now you may be thinking, *Give me a break, dude. I've already got the motivation to pray. I don't need to know* why *I should talk to God; I need to know* how *to make my prayer life as passionate as possible.*

Here's the thing, though. If you aren't praying for the right reasons, you're not even within spitting distance of an intense prayer life. In fact, you may be damaging your relationship with God without even realizing it. So before we move on to the *hows* and *whats* of prayer, let's take care of the *whys*.

To keep this from becoming a five-hundred-page textbook on the dozens of motivations for prayer, we're going to focus our attention on three of the most important reasons to pray. These three deserve special attention because they surface so frequently in the psalms:

1. Forgiveness
2. Guidance
3. Protection

I. forgiveness

Nothing messes up a relationship with God like sin. Every time we give in to temptation, let our emotions get the better of us, put our own needs ahead of others', choose not to obey the Bible, we drive a big, fat wedge between us and God.

That's not to say God totally rejects us when we do something wrong. Remember, Jesus died to pay the price for our sins. If we believe in Him, God will never reject us.

But sin does cause problems in the relationship with God. You can't turn your back on God's will or ignore His Word and then expect everything to be cool in your conversations with Him. Your prayer life won't be right again until you open up to Him about what you've done wrong and ask Him to forgive you.

Nothing is lonelier than being separated from God by sin. But don't just take my word for it. Check out what David, the famous shepherd-psalmist-king, had to say after he screwed up big time in God's eyes. (You'll find the gory details of David's sin in 2 Sam. 11:1–12:23.)

> Have mercy upon me, O God,
> According to Your lovingkindness;
> According to the multitude of Your tender mercies,
> Blot out my transgressions.
> Wash me thoroughly from my iniquity,
> And cleanse me from my sin.
> For I acknowledge my transgressions,
> And my sin is always before me.
> Against You, You only, have I sinned,
> And done this evil in Your sight—
> That You may be found just when You speak,
> And blameless when You judge.
> Behold, I was brought forth in iniquity,
> And in sin my mother conceived me.
> Behold, You desire truth in the inward parts,

And in the hidden part You will make me to know wisdom.
Purge me with hyssop, and I shall be clean;
Wash me, and I shall be whiter than snow.
Make me hear joy and gladness,
That the bones You have broken may rejoice.
Hide Your face from my sins,
And blot out all my iniquities.
Create in me a clean heart, O God,
And renew a steadfast spirit within me.
Do not cast me away from Your presence,
And do not take Your Holy Spirit from me.
Restore to me the joy of Your salvation,
And uphold me by Your generous Spirit.
Then I will teach transgressors Your ways,
And sinners shall be converted to You.
Deliver me from the guilt of bloodshed, O God,
The God of my salvation,
And my tongue shall sing aloud of Your righteousness.
O Lord, open my lips,
And my mouth shall show forth Your praise.
For You do not desire sacrifice, or else I would give it;
You do not delight in burnt offering.
The sacrifices of God are a broken spirit,
A broken and a contrite heart—
These, O God, You will not despise.
Do good in Your good pleasure to Zion;
Build the walls of Jerusalem.
Then You shall be pleased with the sacrifices of righteousness,
With burnt offering and whole burnt offering;
Then they shall offer bulls on Your altar. (Ps. 51)

Now that's some serious repenting.

David wasn't worried about his reputation—what other people were saying about him—or even about his conscience. He was worried about the effect his sin had on his relationship with God ("Against You, You only, have I sinned"). That's why he poured his heart out to the Lord in prayer. He had to know that everything was okay with that friendship before he did anything else.

If you want an amazing prayer life, you need the same extreme attitude toward sin that David had. You can't just say, "Oops, my bad," and leave it at that. You can't rationalize your actions or try to convince yourself that they're not as bad as they seem. You've got to step up and take responsibility for them.

As an example of this, check out the following prayer, which comes from the journal of a youth pastor who committed a rather well-publicized (in his community) sin:

> Father . . . Not only did I humiliate myself and my
> family, I damaged Your ministry . . . I failed those who
> look to me for leadership and direction. (Ironic: I can't
> even warn people not to fall into the same trap, since
> no one would listen to me now.) . . . Everything I
> worked for is destroyed, or nearly [destroyed].

It's also important to approach God with the same sense of wonder and unworthiness that David obviously had. Even though David had probably experienced God's forgiveness dozens of times before, he didn't take it for granted. He didn't come to God with an attitude of "I'm here; this is what I did;

now where's my forgiveness?" It was more like "I can't believe You would forgive someone who sins like I do."

And that's the same kind of attitude you need when you pray for forgiveness. You can't really repent unless you understand and take responsibility for what you've done. The more you leave unspoken, the more

> you don't pray to change God's will; you pray to become part of it.

obstacles you build into your relationship with God.

Notice, too, that David wasn't after a quick fix. He didn't treat prayer like a drive-through car wash where you get a quick soul cleaning and then head off down the road. David seriously wanted to change the way he acted and the decisions he made. In verse 10, he even asked God for a new heart! That same desire for change should be at the core of your prayers for forgiveness.

Oh, by the way, there's one more thing you should know about praying for forgiveness, and it comes from 1 John 1:9: "If we confess our sins, He is faithful and just to forgive us our sins and to cleanse us from all unrighteousness." If you really want forgiveness, you've got it.

2. guidance

(If you're the type of person who marks important passages in the books you read, then get your highlighter or red pen ready because you're going to want to remember the next sentence.)

You don't pray to change God's will; you pray to become part of it.

You may convince yourself you know this principle, but really you don't. Think about some of the things you've prayed for recently. Did they sound anything like these?

- "God, please let Anna find a boyfriend so that she won't be so depressed all the time."
- "Lord, please help my father find a job that pays more than the one he has now."
- "Heavenly Father, please don't let our softball tournament get rained out tomorrow."

On the surface, there doesn't seem to be much wrong with these requests. There's certainly nothing in them that would get you booted from a Bible study or Sunday school class. But look at them a little more closely, and you'll see that they don't give God much room to work.

Isn't it possible that

- a boyfriend may not be what Anna really needs right now?
- God placed your father at his current job for a reason?
- the farmers in your area need rain more than you need good weather for a game?

Here's the deal. If you go to the Lord with a list of specific things that you want Him to do in your life and in the lives of your loved ones, you're really saying, "Why don't You hop in the backseat for a while, God, and let me take the wheel? I know more about what's best for me and my friends and family than You do."

→ HEADS UP

The more room you leave for God to work in your prayer life, the more amazed you'll be at what He does. Here are three stories of Bible characters who received stunning answers to their prayers—solutions that they could not have imagined even on their best day.

Abraham (Gen. 15:1–18:15; 21:1–21)

Abraham wanted a son, an heir to carry on his family line. Year after year he asked God for a son—until about the time of his eighty-sixth birthday. That's when Abraham decided that he knew what was best for his family. To get the heir he wanted, he slept with his wife's slave and got her pregnant. But years later, Abraham's wife, Sarah—his ninety-year-old wife, Sarah—became pregnant.

Moses (Ex. 13:17–14:31)

Moses wanted safety for the millions of Israelites who had followed him out of slavery in Egypt. When the enormous caravan reached the Red Sea, they had no place else to go. Pharaoh and his men were in hot pursuit, determined to recapture or kill their former slaves. Who knows what Moses expected God to do that day? It's a good bet, though, that he didn't expect the miracle he witnessed. God pulled back the waters on both sides of the Red Sea to form a path of dry ground right through the middle of it. Every Israelite made it safely across. And when the Egyptian army tried to follow, God closed the waters and drowned them all.

Shadrach, Meshach, and Abed-Nego (Dan. 3)

The three young Israelites wanted to stand firm as they faced execution for not bowing down to an idol. They might have had a notion that God would save them at the last minute, just as they were about to be thrown into the fiery furnace, but they were prepared to die for their beliefs just the same. What they probably didn't expect was to be saved after they were thrown into the furnace. But that's what God did. He allowed them to walk around inside the furnace without getting so much as a sunburn.

When you consider what God did for Abraham, Moses, and Shadrach, Meshach, and Abed-Nego, do you really want to tell Him what to do with your prayer requests?

The psalmists knew that God's will was always better than any solution they could think up by themselves. That's why you'll find prayers like these scattered throughout the book of Psalms:

You are my rock and my protection.
  For the good of your name, lead me and guide me.
Set me free from the trap they set for me,
  because you are my protection.
I give you my life.
  Save me, LORD, God of truth. (Ps. 31:3–5 NCV)

Teach me to do what you want,
  because you are my God.

Let your good Spirit
   lead me on level ground. (Ps. 143:10 NCV)

The psalmists were saying, "You the Man, God." They laid out their situation before Him and asked, "What do *You* want to do about this, Lord?" And then they asked, "How do You want to use me in this situation?"

That's not to say the psalmists lacked personal preferences about what they wanted to happen. Of course, they had opinions about what should happen! When an enemy started messing with them, they probably fantasized about all kinds of divine punishment. They poured out their hearts to God and often asked Him to punish the wicked.

> Give up your notions of what needs to happen and when, and go with God's flow.

However, they didn't take matters into their own hands. They waited for God's action in His timing. They didn't let their personal preferences get in the way of their prayer lives. They were team players all the way, trusting God for the final decision.

You may think you have a pretty good idea about what's best for you and for others. You don't. You may be tempted to offer God some advice on what He should do in certain situations. You shouldn't. God isn't sitting around waiting for your suggestions. He has a plan in the works, whether you care to recognize it or not.

If you want to be part of God's will, an instrument in His plan, then pray for His guidance. Give up your notions of what needs to happen and when, and go with God's flow. If you're not willing to be a team player, then at least get out of the way (spiritually speaking) so that others who are willing can get things done.

3. protection

We'll let the apostle Peter hammer home the third reason for prayer with his warning in 1 Peter 5:8: "The devil, your enemy, goes around like a roaring lion looking for someone to eat" (NCV).

If these words aren't enough to freak you out at least a little, allow me to give you a more complete picture of what you're up against. The devil is not just a roaring lion. He's a roaring lion who knows exactly where and when you're most vulnerable.

And did I mention that he has an unbelievable arsenal of weapons at his disposal? He can attack you through temptation. If that doesn't work, he can use jealousy. If that doesn't work, he can use anger or bitterness or fear—whatever it takes to beat you.

The only weapons you have to battle him are prayer and Scripture. And if that doesn't seem like a fair fight to you, you're right—it's not. The devil doesn't stand a chance.

You see, if you can develop an extreme prayer life, you'll be equipped to take on the devil, any time and any place, no matter what weapon he's packing.

Get a load of David's words in this psalm:

The LORD is my light and my salvation;
Whom shall I fear?

The LORD is the strength of my life;
Of whom shall I be afraid?
When the wicked came against me
To eat up my flesh,
My enemies and foes,
They stumbled and fell.
Though an army may encamp against me,
My heart shall not fear;
Though war may rise against me,
In this I will be confident.
One thing I have desired of the LORD,
That will I seek:
That I may dwell in the house of the LORD
All the days of my life,
To behold the beauty of the LORD,
And to inquire in His temple.
For in the time of trouble
He shall hide me in His pavilion;
In the secret place of His tabernacle
He shall hide me;
He shall set me high upon a rock.
And now my head shall be lifted up above my
    enemies all around me;
Therefore I will offer sacrifices of joy in His tabernacle;
I will sing, yes, I will sing praises to the LORD.
Hear, O LORD, when I cry with my voice!
Have mercy also upon me, and answer me.
When You said, "Seek My face,"
My heart said to You, "Your face, LORD, I will seek."
Do not hide Your face from me;

Do not turn Your servant away in anger;
You have been my help;
Do not leave me nor forsake me,
O God of my salvation.
When my father and my mother forsake me,
Then the LORD will take care of me.
Teach me Your way, O LORD,
And lead me in a smooth path,
      because of my enemies.
Do not deliver me to the will of my adversaries;
For false witnesses have risen against me,
And such as breathe out violence.
I would have lost heart, unless I had believed
That I would see the goodness of the LORD
In the land of the living.
Wait on the LORD;
Be of good courage,
And He shall strengthen your heart;
Wait, I say, on the LORD! (Ps. 27)

Can't you just picture the psalmist-king strutting confidently through ancient Israel, knowing that the Lord had his back?

Look at those verses again, and you'll see that there's no cockiness, ego, or showboating in them. David wasn't a fool. He knew he wasn't strong enough to deal with the evil in the world on his own. He knew that God was his only hope for defeating temptation and the rest of Satan's weapons.

"The LORD will take care of me" (Ps. 27:10). What better reason is there to turn to Him in prayer as often as possible?

What's it to you?

Where there are dos, you know there have to be some don'ts. We've already discussed three things that should motivate you to pray. Now let's check out a couple of mistakes to avoid when it comes to your reasons for praying.

don't pray to get what you want

God doesn't live in a genie bottle. He doesn't pop out, ready to grant you three wishes whenever you ask for them. Here's a tip: if your prayers resemble a Christmas wish list, you're a long way from a passionate prayer life.

And we're not just talking about material possessions, either. Here are a few more examples:

- "God, please let me make a good impression on my girlfriend's parents so that they won't think I'm a jerk."
- "Lord, please help me find a way to make up the car payments I missed the past two months."
- "Heavenly Father, please don't let me get stuck in this airport on Thanksgiving Day."

Can you see the "me, me, me" at the heart of each of these requests? All of them have to do with making your life easier. The problem is, that may not be what God has in mind for you. He may have some big-time plans to stretch you and pull you out of your comfort zone. But you won't be able to see that if you're too busy checking your list of wants.

Earlier in this chapter I mentioned the importance of becoming a part of God's will instead of trying to change it.

Here's what it comes down to: if you want God to use you in His plan—and if you want to become a passionate pray-er—one of the first things you need to do is to cut out your self-centered prayer requests.

God encourages us to cast all our cares on Him. He wants to hear our most personal thoughts, fears, and dreams. But if we can't see past ourselves, then we can't really become a dynamic part of God's plan. We won't see the needs of others, and we won't notice God at work. One way to broaden your perspective is to pray for understanding. Ask the Lord to help you understand what your needs and the needs of others really are. Ask Him to help you see beyond your immediate circumstances to what He ultimately has in store.

don't pray out of superstition

Some people pray "just to be safe." They're not really convinced that prayer does much good, but they're worried that something might happen if they don't pray. So they throw up a few quick words of thanks, maybe speed through the Lord's Prayer, and then get on with their day.

For them, prayer is like a good-luck charm. Say a prayer, and you'll have a good day. Forget to pray, and watch out. With that attitude it doesn't take long for the ritual of prayer to become more important than the prayer itself. Praying becomes about as spiritually rewarding as brushing your teeth or taking your vitamins.

This "superstitious" attitude not only underestimates the power of prayer, but it also makes God look bad. God isn't motivated by vengeance. He's not going to send a string of bad luck your way to get even with you for forgetting to pray. That's not how He works at all.

Don't forget, prayer is a privilege. If you choose not to take advantage of it, that's your loss. Missing out on an opportunity to talk personally with the Creator of the universe is punishment enough. God's not gonna put a curse on you to rub salt in the wound.

one last thing

Look, there are going to be times when you pray for no other reason than that you feel like it. Depending on the circumstances in your life, good or bad, you may get an overwhelming urge to talk to the One who can help you celebrate, make sense of life, or keep things in their proper perspective.

Go for it. But in your spontaneity, don't lose sight of your motivation for praying.

Remember the One you're talking to.

taking it to heart

Time to put the ol' gray matter to work. Learning to pray for the right reasons is going to take some thought on your part. To help fire up your synapses, consider the following questions:

1. How might praying for the wrong reasons negatively affect your relationship with God?
2. When was the last time you prayed for what might have been the wrong reasons? What were the circumstances?

3. Have you ever prayed for something, knowing that it probably wasn't God's will? If so, why?

4. If someone asked you right now why you pray, what would you say?

5. How will you be able to tell if you start praying for the wrong reasons?

6. How are you going to adjust your prayer life to make sure that your motivation is right? Specifically how can you learn to pray for reasons that will bring you closer to God?

one from the heart

Based on what you've learned about the different motivations for prayer and what you've read of the psalmists' prayers in this chapter, write your own prayer to God. Be sure to share your thoughts and feelings about why you want to communicate with Him. And try to be as specific as possible throughout your prayer.

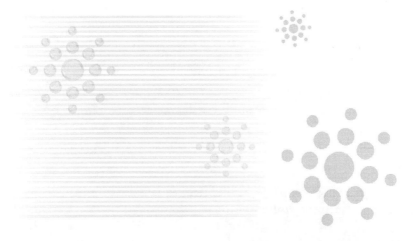

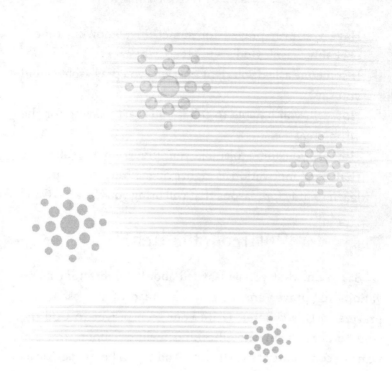

2

DO YOU KNOW THE ONE YOU'RE TALKING TO?

Justin felt beads of sweat forming on his forehead. Somebody had to start a conversation soon. The silence was getting seriously awkward. Why did I ever agree to a blind date? he asked himself for the fiftieth time that night.

The waiter handed out the menus and went to fetch drinks. "Hope you like steak," Justin said. "Everyone says this is the best steak place in town."

"Actually I'm a vegetarian," Kacy replied. "I have a real problem with people killing another creature just because they like the taste of its flesh."

"Uh . . . okay," Justin said as he scanned the menu, hoping to find some entrée that didn't have meat in it. But this was a steak place—period. No pasta, no vegetable plate—not even a dinner salad anywhere on the menu. Just meat and potatoes.

"Uh, well, we could go to another restaurant," he suggested.

"It's Saturday night," Kacy reminded him. "We'd never get

a table before nine o'clock. I'll just have a baked potato, I guess."

At the next table, a baby started screaming. Justin waited for a few moments for the tantrum to stop. But it didn't. After three or four minutes, he rolled his eyes and motioned for the waiter. "The least I can do is get us a table in the 'No screaming brats' section," he joked.

"I love kids," Kacy responded with a cold glare. "I work as a volunteer at the children's hospital. I don't have a problem with a little screaming."

Way to go, dude, Justin told himself. *Now she thinks you're a baby-hating animal killer.*

Justin decided to try the one area of common ground he knew they had: Derek—Justin's friend and Kacy's coworker—the one who had set up the date. "You must have a blast working with Derek. I've known him since my freshman year of high school. He's a good guy."

"You think so?" Kacy asked. "If he's such a good guy, why did he lie about me to our boss just to get a promotion?"

"Um . . . well, I don't know," Justin said. He was now officially 0 for 3 in the conversation department. He stole a quick glance at his watch: 7:20. He felt a knot tighten in the pit of his stomach. They'd been together only twenty minutes, but it felt like twenty years.

Why did I ever agree to a blind date? he asked himself for the fifty-first time.

it's like this

If you've ever been on a blind date, you probably have a few horror stories of your own. After all, what's more awkward than trying to make conversation with someone you don't know very well, especially when it's just the two of you?

You can't really talk about anything deep or meaningful— you're practically strangers. You also have to worry about saying the wrong thing or giving the wrong impression. Even worse, you don't know which topics are off-limits or what might set the other person off and ruin the whole experience.

if you want maximum power from your prayer life, you've got to put maximum effort into it.

So usually what happens is that you end up talking about nothing and waiting for the whole thing to be over.

Strange as it may seem, the same thing can happen with prayer if you're not careful.

If you don't know—really know—the One you're communicating with when you pray, you may find yourself talking about nothing and waiting for the whole thing to be over. Your prayer time may not be as awkward as a bad blind date, but it probably won't mean much to you. You may even feel that you're just going through the motions. And what's worse, your prayers probably won't accomplish much.

That's not the kind of prayer life you want, is it? (If it were, then you wouldn't be reading this book.)

No, what you want is to experience dynamic prayer—the kind of prayer that changes lives and makes a difference in the world. But to develop that kind of prayer life, you have to get to know the One you're talking to. And not just in a casual, "Hey, God, how's it going?" way, either.

If you want maximum power from your prayer life, you've

got to put maximum effort into it. That means you have to get to know God better than you know your best friend, better than you know your family—even better than you know yourself. Your goal is to understand who God is, what He's capable of, why He does what He does, and what's important to Him.

If that doesn't seem like a monster responsibility to you, then you probably don't have the complete picture of what we're talking about. Think about how long it took you to get to know your best friend. What kinds of things did you have to learn about him or her? What mistakes did you make on your way to best friendship? How long was it before you were comfortable sharing your most private thoughts and feelings with each other?

Now think about how that same process might work with God. Keep in mind that He's been around forever. He's had His hand in every moment of human history. He sees everything and knows everything.

This isn't Someone you're going to get to know overnight.

You can start to gather bits of information about Him—information that you can use like pieces of a jigsaw puzzle as you try to put together the big picture of who God is.

→ **HEADS UP**

The good news is that you can find everything you need to know about God in your Bible. In fact, the Bible is like God's résumé. Open it to almost any page, and you'll find something either about God or related to Him.

With so much information to plow through, you may have a problem deciding where to begin. Here are just a few highlights to get you started in your quest to understand who God is and what He's like:

- God created the universe and everything in it (Gen. 1).
- God made a special covenant with Abraham and promised to make him into a great nation (Gen. 12:1–3).
- God revealed His supreme holiness to Isaiah (Isa. 6:1–10).
- God revealed His own name to Moses (Ex. 3).
- God sacrificed His only Son to pay the penalty for our sins and give us the chance to spend eternity with Him (John 3:1–21).
- God prepared a place for His followers to join Him in heaven (John 14:1–7).

Now before we go any farther in this chapter, you have a chance to bail. If you're okay with the idea of having a casual relationship with God—if knowing a little about Him is enough for you—you might as well stop reading right now. And don't just skip to the next chapter, either. Just put the book down for good.

If you're not interested in building a relationship with God that's so deep and so meaningful it makes all of your other friendships look like jokes, then you won't find anything in the rest of this book that will help you salvage your prayer life.

On the other hand, if you're willing to commit yourself to

learning everything you can about God—who He is, what He's done, what pleases Him, what upsets Him, what He expects from His people—you've taken the first major step toward becoming a solid prayer warrior.

If that's what you're striving for, keep reading. Let the psalmists take you to school.

Word

Asaph is not what you'd call a major player in the Bible. We know that he was a worship leader in Israel and that he wrote a few psalms, but that's about it. The only other thing we know about him is that he really knew God. This guy was tight with the heavenly Father. All you need to do is to look at his prayer in Psalm 77 to know that.

It goes a little something like this:

I cried out to God with my voice—
To God with my voice;
And He gave ear to me.
In the day of my trouble I sought the Lord;
My hand was stretched out in the night without ceasing;
My soul refused to be comforted.
I remembered God, and was troubled;
I complained, and my spirit was overwhelmed. Selah
You hold my eyelids open;
I am so troubled that I cannot speak.
I have considered the days of old,
The years of ancient times.
I call to remembrance my song in the night;

I meditate within my heart,
And my spirit makes diligent search.
Will the Lord cast off forever?
And will He be favorable no more?
Has His mercy ceased forever?
Has His promise failed forevermore?
Has God forgotten to be gracious?
Has He in anger shut up His tender mercies? Selah
And I said, "This is my anguish;
But I will remember the years of the right hand
    of the Most High."
I will remember the works of the LORD;
Surely I will remember Your wonders of old.
I will also meditate on all Your work,
And talk of Your deeds.
Your way, O God, is in the sanctuary;
Who is so great a God as our God?
You are the God who does wonders;
You have declared Your strength among the peoples.
You have with Your arm redeemed Your people,
The sons of Jacob and Joseph. Selah
The waters saw You, O God;
The waters saw You, they were afraid;
The depths also trembled.
The clouds poured out water;
The skies sent out a sound;
Your arrows also flashed about.
The voice of Your thunder was in the whirlwind;
The lightnings lit up the world;
The earth trembled and shook.

Your way was in the sea,
Your path in the great waters,
And Your footsteps were not known.
You led Your people like a flock
By the hand of Moses and Aaron.

There's some serious emotion going down in this prayer. These aren't the kinds of things you'd talk about with just anybody. What you've got in Psalm 77 is someone pouring out his soul to his closest friend and most trusted adviser.

Asaph was so familiar with God—and so comfortable with talking to Him—that he wasn't even afraid to question the Lord in the midst of his depression ("Has God forgotten to be gracious?"). Asaph knew God wouldn't be offended by his questions. He knew that because he knew God.

If all you knew of God were the stories of His judgment and destruction, you might be afraid to talk to Him the way Asaph did in his prayer. You might worry about getting zapped with a lightning bolt right between the eyes.

But Asaph wasn't worried. He knew God wouldn't punish him for speaking his mind and sharing his deepest feelings.

You know how you can say things to your best friend that you wouldn't dream of saying to someone else? That's the way Asaph was with God. He was completely comfortable talking to the Lord about anything.

Asaph had an awesome prayer life. Good for him.

And good for us.

You see, we can get some clues from Asaph's prayer about what God is like—clues that will help us as we work on our own close relationship with Him. In Psalm 77, Asaph dropped hints about three characteristics of God that are important for us to understand if we want to have an extreme prayer life.

Here are the clues Asaph left for us when he wrote down his prayer:

1. God has the power to do anything.
2. God listens.
3. God has a plan.

These may seem like simple statements, but they're not. Each one carries an important truth that can make or break your prayer life. Let's examine them one at a time to see what we can learn about God and our communication with Him.

I. God has the power to do anything

If you're like most people, you probably didn't think twice when you read the subtitle above. It's one of those things we just take for granted. Fire is hot, ice is cold, the Chicago Cubs stink, and God is all-powerful.

But glancing back at Asaph's prayer, you'll find that the psalmist didn't take God's power for granted. Nowhere in Psalm 77 will you find a lame generalization like, "God, You are so powerful, blah, blah, blah." A person who doesn't know God very well would say something like that.

Asaph wanted to focus on the specifics of God's power. Not only did he know of incidents where God demonstrated His power; he knew the details of those incidents.

For this prayer, Asaph chose to focus on God's work in leading the Israelites out of slavery in Egypt. If you've read the book of Exodus lately or if you've seen the movie *The Ten*

Commandments on TV, you know what happened. When the Israelites reached the Red Sea with the Egyptian army hot on their trail, it looked like the end of the line. There was nowhere for them to go.

That's when God parted the water, giving the Israelites a path to walk on dry ground right through the middle of the sea. After the Israelites made it safely to the other side, God let the waters go, destroying the entire Egyptian army.

Now that's power.

And Asaph knew about it because he'd taken the time to learn about God. He was able to talk specifics because he cared enough to study God's résumé.

Asaph was not only praising God for what He had done, but he was also taking comfort in it. Asaph knew that if God was powerful enough to hold back the waters of the Red Sea, He was capable of helping him through any situation, no matter how hopeless things seemed.

2. God listens

You can tell from the tone of Asaph's prayer that he and God had been close friends. They had a history together. When Asaph hit rock bottom in his personal life, the first place he turned to was God.

Because he knew God would listen.

You think this was Asaph's first prayer? Of course not. No rookie could ever come up with something as deep and personal as Psalm 77. Asaph was a prayer veteran.

He wasn't just throwing requests out into the cosmic void, hoping they would be heard. He knew he was talking one-on-one with a Friend. What's more, he knew that Friend was listening closely to his every word ("I cried out to God with my voice . . . and He gave ear to me").

How cool is that? To know that the One who holds the entire universe together will give you His full attention anytime you feel like talking. Talk about knowing people in high places.

It's obvious that Asaph didn't take his privilege lightly, though. The tone of his prayer suggests that he was humbled by the Almighty's attention. He wasn't walking around in a tunic with the words *God listens to me* stitched across the back.

The same goes for the anonymous author of Psalm 66. He spoke about God's listening skills:

> Come and hear, all you who fear God,
> And I will declare what He has done for my soul.
> I cried to Him with my mouth,
> And He was extolled with my tongue.
> If I regard iniquity in my heart,
> The Lord will not hear.
> But certainly God has heard me;
> He has attended to the voice of my prayer.
> Blessed be God,
> Who has not turned away my prayer,
> Nor His mercy from me! (vv. 16–20)

David, another psalmist, who also happened to be king of Israel, was amazed by the idea that God paid attention to him. You can almost hear his jaw dropping in the following passage:

> O Lord, our Lord,
> How excellent is Your name in all the earth,

Who have set Your glory above the heavens!
Out of the mouth of babes and nursing infants
You have ordained strength,
Because of Your enemies,
That You may silence the enemy and the avenger.
When I consider Your heavens, the work of Your fingers,
The moon and the stars, which You have ordained,
What is man that You are mindful of him,
And the son of man that You visit him?
For You have made him a little lower than the angels,
And You have crowned him with glory and honor. (Ps. 8:1–5)

David was so blown away by the concept of a listening God that he gave the Lord a special nickname: "You who hear prayer" (Ps. 65:2). (Okay, maybe it's not as cool a name as Blink or Chief—but you've got to admit, it's a lot better than "You who could care less about what we say.")

Have you ever talked to someone who you knew wasn't listening to you? You can see it in his eyes, can't you? That moment when the brain clicks off and starts wandering elsewhere. It's usually followed by an automatic head nod and an occasional repetition of the syllables "uh-huh."

And once the person's attention has wandered, there's not much you can do to get it back. Even if you were to say something like, "My nose hair caught fire when a psychotic monkey shot a flamethrower at me," the most you could probably hope for is a vacant stare and a halfhearted "uh-huh."

If you had a friend whose attention wandered off to La-La Land every time you had something to say, how long would you keep going to that person to talk? Chances are, you would probably start searching for a better conversation partner pretty soon.

Though the psalmists obviously had a lot to say—there are 150 psalms in the Bible—they weren't worried about God's losing interest in their words. They were convinced that as long as they wanted to talk, God wanted to listen. Deep in their souls, the psalmists could feel His interest and concern. That's what kept them coming back to Him with their prayers.

> God listens when we speak, no matter what we have to say to him or how difficult it is for us to spit out the words.

Now, a lot of things have changed in the past three thousand years, but God isn't one of them. What was true for the psalmists is true for us. God listens when we speak, no matter what we have to say to Him or how difficult it is for us to spit out the words.

3. God has a plan

Even though Asaph knew God, you get the feeling from Psalm 77 that he didn't always understand what God was doing. But that didn't keep him from placing his faith in his heavenly Father. Asaph knew that God had something awesome in store for his life. So even in the midst of serious depression, he could say to God—and to himself—"I know You've got better things ahead for me."

How could Asaph be so sure? Apparently because he'd seen evidence of God's plan in the past. And we're not just talking about historical events like the Israelites' Red Sea miracle, either. The statement in verse 11, "I will remember the works of the LORD," has a personal ring to it. Asaph knew that no situation was hopeless if he just allowed God's will to work itself out.

The Lord Himself revealed a little about His plans in Psalm 32 when He interrupted David's praise to make a few things clear. Here is what He had to say:

> I will instruct you and teach you in the way you should go;
> I will guide you with My eye.
> Do not be like the horse or like the mule,
> Which have no understanding,
> Which must be harnessed with bit and bridle,
> Else they will not come near you. (Ps. 32:8–9)

Asaph, David, and the rest of the psalmists recognized that God's plan was all they needed for their lives. They knew God well enough to know that trusting and following His will was the smartest thing they could do—regardless of whether they understood it or not.

What's it to you?

All right, maybe you learned something new about God in this chapter, and maybe you didn't. The question now is, What do these three characteristics—the fact that God is powerful, that He listens to us, and that He has a plan— have to do with an extreme prayer life?

Glad you asked.

If you will take these characteristics to heart and put

some serious thought into what they really mean, you'll find that you can approach prayer a little differently from the way you're used to. Specifically you'll find that you can be a little more

bold,

purposeful,

aware,

in the way you communicate with your heavenly Father.

be bold

If you don't take advantage of the opportunities that arise from God's power, then you might as well tattoo a big *L* on your forehead because you are losing out, big time. Specifically, you're missing out on a chance to make a real difference in your life, in the lives of your friends and family members, and in the world.

Knowing what you know about God's strength should encourage you to be bold and ambitious in your prayers. If you have access to the kind of power that defies nature, why would you be content to focus on only piddly little things such as tests and job interviews?

That's not to say you should avoid taking little things to God. You should take such things to Him. But why stop there? We're talking about mind-boggling power here. Why not stretch your requests to include your church, your state, your country, and the world?

What's stopping you from taking world-changing requests to God? When the Israelites were freed from slavery, world history was changed. Who's to say that God won't do that again—as the result of your prayers?

Asaph, David, and the other psalmists weren't shy about asking God for major things. They were always going to Him with urgent requests for their nation. They knew what God was capable of, and they wanted His power at work in their country.

be purposeful

The fact that God listens to your prayer is not just a comfort; it's also a responsibility. Think of it this way: If you have the Creator of the universe on the line, listening to everything you say, wouldn't you want to make the most of the opportunity?

Knowing that they had an attentive audience allowed the psalmists to go into great detail in their prayers. Knowing that God still listens today gives you the same luxury.

If you're striving for a fulfilling prayer life, forget about those meaningless quickie prayers that you recite from memory without really considering what you're saying. Make sure that you have reasons for every request you offer to God. Talk to Him about those reasons. Be specific about what you're thankful for.

In other words, give God something meaningful to listen to.

be aware

God has a plan not only for your life, but also for the lives of the people around you. Don't forget that when you pray. You may think you know what's best for everyone involved in your prayers.

Get over yourself.

If you know God—really know Him—then you know that His ways are perfect. And since nothing beats perfection, there's no chance that your way is better than His. Deal with it.

From a more positive standpoint, you can do what the psalmists did and take comfort in God's perfect plans. When things got bad—really bad—for Asaph, David, and their psalm teammates, they told God about it in no uncertain terms. They gave Him details about all of the bad things that were going on in their lives. Sometimes they questioned why He would let such things happen to them.

But they always came back to one important point: You know what You're doing, God, so I'll just trust in You. I may not understand Your plan, but I know it's perfect, so I'll just ride out the storm until I can see things more clearly.

If you think that's an easy thing to say, then think again. It takes a boatload of faith to turn things over to God, especially when you're depressed or your enemies are hounding you. But if you really, really believe that God's plan is perfect (based on what you know about Him), then you can do it.

Did you catch those last four words? *You* can do it.

The psalmists weren't spiritual superheroes. Their prayers allow us to see that they struggled with the same doubts and fears that all of us struggle with. Spiritually speaking, they weren't much different from us. So if they were able to put aside their doubts and fears and remind themselves that God has a perfect plan working, you can do it too.

That doesn't mean you have to censor your prayers. Say whatever's on your mind. If you want God to help you

get rid of an ex who won't leave you alone,

afford a new house or car,

become successful at your chosen career,

then tell Him.

But don't stop there. After you've poured out your heart, start looking at things from His perspective. Try to see what His will is, then give yourself over to it. And if you can't see His will, then give yourself over to it anyway. You won't be sorry.

one last thing

Getting to know God is a lifelong adventure. It's like peeling an onion—one layer leads to another. You may think you have a grasp of who He is until the next layer reveals something about Him that you never expected.

One thing is certain, though. The deeper you go in your exploration of God, the stronger—and more extreme—your prayer life will become.

taking it to heart

Time to put the ol' gray matter to work. Developing an intimate relationship with God could lead to some big changes in your life. To help you prepare for some of those changes, think through the following questions. If an extreme prayer life is your goal, you'll need to put some serious, final-exam-level thought into your answers.

1. What's the most surprising thing you've ever learned about God? Why did it come as such a surprise to you?
2. What misconceptions about God have messed up your prayer life in the past? How did (or will) you get beyond those misconceptions?
3. Of all the Bible stories you know about God, which ones

mean the most to you personally? Why are those stories so important to you?

4. Write down three questions about God—who He is, what He's like, and so on—for which you would like to have answers.

5. Write down the names of three mature Christians whom you can go to for answers to those questions.

6. Write down three things you can do this week to start building a more meaningful relationship with God.

7. What changes are you going to make to your prayer life as a result of getting to know God more intimately? Specifically how can you be more bold, purposeful, and aware in your prayers?

One from the heart

Based on what you've learned about God and what you've read of the psalmists' prayers in this chapter, write your own prayer to God. Be sure to share your thoughts and feelings about who He is and what He's done. And try to be as specific as possible throughout your prayer.

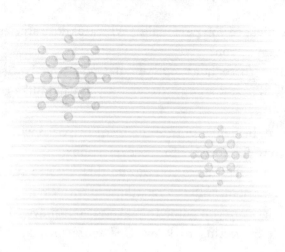

3

AND HOW

The worship leader lifted his arms dramatically and turned his face heavenward. Megan and Calista bowed their heads with the rest of the congregation. In a voice that echoed throughout the sanctuary, the worship leader began, "O heavenly Father, You who created and sustain all . . ."

"How much time do you think he spends practicing these prayers?" Megan whispered.

Calista looked over at her, shrugged, and bowed her head again.

" . . . Your power defies understanding, Your love defies comprehension . . ."

"And how long do you think it takes him to write them?" Megan whispered.

Calista held her finger to her lips, but didn't open her eyes. Be quiet.

" . . . will not be afraid, for in the midst of the hurricane, You are there; in the darkest night, You are there; and in . . ."

"You know he has to write them because nobody talks like that off the top of his head," Megan continued in her quietest voice.

Calista gave her a stern look and nodded her head once for emphasis. I mean it. Shut up.

" . . . and, from the depths of Your mercy and grace, Your Spirit comforts and convicts us so that . . ."

"Unless he has a thesaurus or something up there where we can't see it," Megan whispered.

Calista gave her a quick elbow to the ribs. You're asking for it.

" . . . with the unimpeachable assurance that our suffering is not in vain, nor is it . . ."

"Maybe he hires professional prayer writers to do the work for him, and then he just comes out and performs them."

Calista gave Megan another elbow to the ribs, and this time kept it there. If you don't shut up, you're going home with bruised ribs.

" . . . and may Your Word fall on the fertile soil of our hearts, bringing forth fruit from the seeds that were planted . . ."

"Man, his prayers are way better than mine," Megan said quietly. *"I wonder if God likes listening to him better than He likes listening to me."*

"I know I do!" Calista hissed before giving Megan a sharp kick to the shins.

" . . . and we will give You all the honor and glory. In the name of our Lord Jesus Christ, we pray. Amen."

it's like this

The next thing we have to discuss is how to pray. But don't get the wrong impression. It's not like there's one specific way to pray that you need to memorize. God doesn't judge your prayer performance. You won't get points deducted for opening your eyes in the middle of a prayer or for forgetting to say, "In Jesus' name," before "Amen." How boring would that be if every prayer had to follow one rigid set of guidelines? ("Place your hands together and hold them at a forty-five-degree angle to the floor . . . Always begin your prayer with 'Our heavenly Father.' . . . Your praise-to-request ratio should be no less than 3 to 1.")

The great thing about prayer is that you don't need any special knowledge or skills to get started. You don't have to learn an ancient language. You don't have to memorize any secret codes. You don't have to enter any passwords to get "on-line." You just say the words, and God listens.

Simple, right? Well, yes . . . and no.

If that's all you needed to know about prayer, this chapter would be ending right about here. But if you flip ahead in this book, you'll see that there are still plenty of pages left to go. So there must be something more.

Here's the thing. The bow-your-head-and-say-whatever-comes-to-mind method of prayer is okay for beginners. But your prayers, like every other area of your Christian walk, must mature over time. "Now I lay me down to sleep" works for a four-year-old but not for an adult.

Prayer is a skill. To master it, you need to practice it. The more you practice, the better you get. Practice, in this case, involves more than just spending time talking to God, though. It also involves learning from the prayer experiences and practices of other believers.

In the book of Psalms alone, you'll discover many prayer

styles. Spend enough time studying them, and you may be able to find something in each style that you can apply to your prayer life.

Of course, these prayer styles and strategies won't exactly leap off your Bible's pages at you. You won't notice any headings that read "David's Seven Tips for Quality Prayer" or "Asaph's Recipe for God-Pleasing Prayers." The psalmists wrote what they felt. They weren't thinking about passing on prayer advice to future generations. If we're going to learn anything from them, we need to search their words.

Word

If you spend any amount of quality time in the book of Psalms, then you're going to find many prayer examples to follow. To give you a head start in your search, I've identified four of them. If your goal is to become a passionate pray-er, you will need to think about these types of prayer:

1. Creative prayer
2. Unique prayer
3. Persistent prayer
4. Frequent prayer

Let's take a look at each of them.

I. creative prayer

How seriously do you take your prayers? How much time do you spend in preparation before you actually start talking to God? If you're like a lot of Christians, you might have answered, "Very seriously," to the first question and, "Huh?" to the second.

The idea of preparing to pray may not have crossed your mind. When it's time to pray, you just open your mouth and let it rip. After all, isn't prayer a spontaneous thing?

Not the way the psalmists looked at it.

A quick stroll through the book of Psalms will give you an idea of how important it was to the psalmists to get their prayers just right. Though some of the psalms are similar in style and wording, all of them have characteristics that set them apart.

The author of Psalm 117 said everything he needed to say in 2 verses. The author of Psalm 119 took 176 verses to communicate his thoughts and feelings to God. But that's not all. As an added challenge, the author of Psalm 119 designed his prayer as an acrostic. For each of the 22 consonants in the Hebrew alphabet, there are 8 verses that begin with that letter. How long do you think that took to write?

The psalmists seem to have done their best not to repeat themselves in prayer. In trying to keep their prayers fresh and interesting, they drew on the creativity and imagination that the Lord had given them.

To give you an idea of this creativity, pay attention to the images and language in the following passage:

> For my days are consumed like smoke,
> And my bones are burned like a hearth.
> My heart is stricken and withered like grass,
> So that I forget to eat my bread.
> Because of the sound of my groaning
> My bones cling to my skin.
> I am like a pelican of the wilderness;

I am like an owl of the desert.
I lie awake,
And am like a sparrow alone on the housetop. (Ps. 102:3–7)

By drawing on his knowledge of nature and choosing just the right words, the psalmist was able to create a "visual" prayer. You can actually "see" what he's saying and how he feels. In case you're wondering, pelicans, owls, and sparrows live in isolated, lonely places.

The psalmist could have said, "Heavenly Father, I feel lonely." It would have had the same meaning. But it wouldn't have been the same prayer. The psalmist chose instead to go the extra mile and spice up his prayer with images that the Lord would appreciate. He wanted to bring something creative and different to his conversation with God.

Along those same lines, get a load of this description of the Almighty:

The LORD reigns;
Let the earth rejoice;
Let the multitude of isles be glad!
Clouds and darkness surround Him;
Righteousness and justice are
　　　the foundation of His throne.
A fire goes before Him,
And burns up His enemies round about.
His lightnings light the world;
The earth sees and trembles.
The mountains melt like wax at the presence of the LORD,
At the presence of the Lord of the whole earth.

The heavens declare His righteousness,
And all the peoples see His glory. (Ps. 97:1–6)

Melting mountains? Now that's a creative prayer. The psalmist could have conveyed a similar sentiment by saying, "Lord, You are so powerful." But that wasn't good enough for him. He wanted to find the best, most creative way to express God's power that he could imagine.

> your prayers should reflect exactly who you are, where you are in your life, and what you want in your relationship with God—without any pretenses or fakeness.

Does God demand that kind of creativity in every prayer? Of course not. Does He appreciate the extra effort that goes into creative prayers? What do you think? (Hint: Look at the prayers He chose to include in His Word.)

2. unique prayer

Unique doesn't necessarily mean "weird" or "unusual." It means "one of a kind." Your prayers should reflect your personal situation, your style of talking, your true emotional state, your individual way of looking at the world, your distinctive method of showing gratitude, and so on. Your prayers should reflect exactly who you are, where you are in your life, and what you want in your relationship with God—without any pretenses or fakeness.

I keep throwing the prayers of the psalmists in your face, but not because I want you to duplicate what they did. You can learn a lot from other people's prayer styles, but you shouldn't copy them. Instead, you want to develop a style of your own—one that suits your unique situation.

To give you an idea of what I mean, let's consider a prayer David wrote during a very bad time in his life. David actually thought he was dying when he wrote the following words:

> O LORD, do not rebuke me in Your anger,
> Nor chasten me in Your hot displeasure.
> Have mercy on me, O LORD, for I am weak;
> O LORD, heal me, for my bones are troubled.
> My soul also is greatly troubled;
> But You, O LORD—how long?
> Return, O LORD, deliver me!
> Oh, save me for Your mercies' sake!
> For in death there is no remembrance of You;
> In the grave who will give You thanks?
> I am weary with my groaning;
> All night I make my bed swim;
> I drench my couch with my tears.
> My eye wastes away because of grief;
> It grows old because of all my enemies.
> Depart from me, all you workers of iniquity;
> For the LORD has heard the voice of my weeping.
> The LORD has heard my supplication;
> The LORD will receive my prayer.
> Let all my enemies be ashamed and greatly troubled;
> Let them turn back and be ashamed suddenly. (Ps. 6:1–10)

David included personal details in this prayer: "I am weak," "my bones are troubled," "I drench my couch with my tears," and "my eye wastes away because of grief."

To get a more modern spin on this type of prayer, check out this excerpt from the journal of a man who had just lost his second child to miscarriage in the space of a year:

> O God, this is killing me . . . The first [miscarriage] was bad enough, but I got through it because I kept telling myself that You were strengthening our faith through the tough times. But two in a row just seems cruel . . . I'm not sure that I can face this pain again tomorrow. This sick feeling in my stomach won't go away. All day I feel like I've been walking hunched over, almost like there's this invisible weight pressing down on me . . . Somebody said I have to be strong for [my wife] now, but I don't feel very strong. Just numb . . . . Please just give me and [my wife] the strength to get through tomorrow. That's all I'm asking—one day.

There's nothing especially fancy about this prayer. The author didn't try to copy David's style of mourning in Psalm 6. He wasn't trying to impress God with his eloquence. He also didn't try to generalize his experience by saying, "God, please help me through this situation." He gave God the details of his unique situation and his one-of-a-kind feelings. Even his request to "get through tomorrow" reflects the author's unique needs.

Keep in mind that great prayer is rarely general. The closer you get to God, the more you're going to want to get personal and unique in your conversations with Him.

3. persistent prayer

Developing a unique prayer style doesn't mean you have to overhaul your list of requests every time you talk to God. Most extreme pray-ers will tell you that they have at least a couple of requests that they've been taking to God every day for years—even decades!

If that seems to be a bad strategy to you, check out how David seems to have felt about asking God for the same thing again and again:

> Let all my enemies be ashamed and greatly troubled;
> Let them turn back and be ashamed suddenly. (Ps. 6:10)

> I will call upon the LORD, who is worthy to be praised;
> So shall I be saved from my enemies. (Ps. 18:3)

> O my God, I trust in You;
> Let me not be ashamed;
> Let not my enemies triumph over me. (Ps. 25:2)

> My enemies speak evil of me:
> "When will he die, and his name perish?" (Ps. 41:5)

> For the enemy has persecuted my soul;
> He has crushed my life to the ground;
> He has made me dwell in darkness,
> Like those who have long been dead.
> Therefore my spirit is overwhelmed within me;
> My heart within me is distressed.
> (Ps. 143:3–4)

David showed his persistence by continually asking God for the same request. He had faith that God would answer. You can't swing a stick in the book of Psalms without hitting a verse where someone is asking God to do something about his enemies.

You'd think that after a while God would say, "Enough of the enemy stuff! I'm tired of hearing about it day in and day out. Take a hint, dude, and move on with your life." But that's not what God does. The fact that He includes these prayers in the Bible tells us that He doesn't mind repeated requests.

Remember, God has His own time line for doing things. When we bring certain requests to Him, He may smile and say to Himself, "That's not going to happen yet, but if you keep asking, you'll get the answer you're looking for in 1,462 days."

HEADS UP

For another example of God's attitude toward persistent prayer, read the parable of the judge and the widow in Luke 18:1–8. The widow asked the judge to make sure that justice was done in a situation involving her enemies. At first, the judge ignored her request. But the woman continued to ask him for justice. Finally he got tired of her nagging and granted her request. After telling the story, Jesus explained that if an insensitive judge will respond to a poor widow's continual requests, then God will certainly respond to our continual prayer requests.

Now remember, sometimes persistent prayer just won't be cool with God. For example, it's no good if you're asking for something that goes against God's will. If you're praying every day to, say, win the lottery, God's probably going to get tired of hearing it. The more you dwell on inappropriate prayer requests, the less extreme your prayer life is going to be.

The other situation in which persistent prayer might get you in trouble is praying out of laziness. For example, if you pray every day for your best friend to become a Christian but you never make an effort to share your faith with him, God may answer your prayer, but He won't be pleased that your heart is not in it.

But if you feel confident that your prayers are within God's will, and if you're willing to back up your requests with action, then there's no reason that you can't pray for the same thing day after day until God answers your prayer. Most prayer requests don't have expiration dates.

4. frequent prayer

With your busy schedule, how much time can you set aside for prayer? Half an hour a day? Fifteen minutes? The Bible doesn't specify a minimum amount, so we're on our own when it comes to creating a prayer schedule.

David seems to have preferred three-a-days:

> As for me, I will call upon God,
> And the LORD shall save me.
> Evening and morning and at noon
> I will pray, and cry aloud,
> And He shall hear my voice. (Ps. 55:16–17)

We don't know whether this number included just his regularly scheduled prayer times or whether it was an esti-mate of the number of times he talked to God, formally or informally, in the course of a day.

Either way, the fact that David prayed three times a day (or more) doesn't mean we have to. David's schedule might have allowed him to have three uninterrupted times during the day when he could chat with God. You may not have that same luxury.

Whatever your sched-ule allows, the important thing is that you spend as much scheduled time with God as possible. Praying whenever you think of it or whenever you feel that you "need" it just isn't good enough. Passionate pray-ers give prayer the same (or higher) priority as working, going to school, working out, or anything else on their schedules.

> if your relationship with the lord is a priority in your life, your schedule should reflect that.

To become an extreme pray-er, you need to carve out time in your day in which you do nothing but pray. If your relationship with the Lord is a priority in your life, your schedule should reflect that. Obviously, the more time you set aside, the more quickly your prayer life will mature and the more positive results you'll see.

In between your scheduled prayer times, too, you can turn to God for quickie conversations or extra boosts of encouragement or peace of mind. You don't even need to make an appointment!

And if you really want to get into it, pay attention to

what the apostle Paul suggested: "Pray without ceasing" (1 Thess. 5:17). That would be like installing a DSL between you and God. The link would always be open, and information would be continuously flowing back and forth at all hours of the day.

That's what you call *extreme*, extreme prayer.

What's it to you?

Nobody is telling you that you have to live up to the example of the psalmists. Those guys were all-star pray-ers. How fair would it be to judge your prayers or prayer habits against theirs? But you should do everything you can to improve the way you communicate with God. Here are a couple of ideas for you to think about.

experiment with different prayer styles

You do not want to get into a rut in your prayer life. Passionate prayer is not saying the same things to God in the same way again and again. If you want to go the extreme, you have to step outside your comfort zone.

Before you can do that, though, you have to expand your idea of what prayer is. For example, you might try a prayer session in which you don't say a word. Spend a half hour just listening to God. Or instead of telling God how great He is, express your feelings in a drawing, painting, or song. Put your natural talents to work.

Write an acrostic prayer, as the author of Psalm 119 did. Come up with an analogy that expresses your personal feelings, as the author of Psalm 102 did. Create a Top 10 list of the things you appreciate most about God. Better yet, think of your own ideas to spice up your prayers. You don't have to be a creative genius to improve the way you communicate with God. You just need the desire to go beyond the usual methods.

be expressive

Reread David's words in Psalm 6. His emotions seem to bleed off the page. It's almost as if he tapped into the deepest part of his soul and just let everything pour out. If he'd been talking to a friend or family member, he most likely would have held back some of his more personal feelings. But since no one was listening but God, David felt comfortable with letting everything go.

David's complete openness is a great example for all extreme pray-ers. Look, no one's saying it's easy to reveal your deepest thoughts and emotions. Come on now. It's not even easy to admit them to yourself sometimes. But if you're willing to risk being vulnerable, if you're willing to expose everything that's inside you to the Lord, then you'll be able to experience for yourself the kind of comfort and healing that David and the rest of the psalmist team experienced.

Your two biggest enemies in trying to be more expressive in your prayers are denial and self-consciousness. If you're trying to maintain a certain appearance—for others or for yourself—then you may not want to face the fears, insecurities, jealousies, or hurts you feel deep down. And if you're naturally shy and reserved, you may be embarrassed to talk about such personal things, even to God.

The key, then, is to start small. Find one emotion that

you're comfortable talking about, and begin with that. Then the next time you pray, find an emotion that's a bit more difficult to bring up, and try talking about that.

Once you get used to the idea of making yourself vulnerable before God, you'll pray at a more intense level than you may have imagined was possible.

one last thing

A key to becoming an extreme pray-er is never being satisfied with your status quo. No matter how good you may think your prayer life is right now, keep tweaking, trying new things, and doing whatever you can to continually improve your communication with God.

That doesn't mean you should load up your prayer time with gimmicks, though. Your efforts to be creative and expressive in your prayers should not distract you from your ultimate goal of developing an intimate relationship with God and finding your place in His will. But as you discover new ways to communicate with the Father, your prayer time will become more exciting, more open, and more fulfilling.

taking it to heart

Time to put the ol' gray matter to work. Making creative changes to your prayer life won't exactly be a snap. You've got some work on your hands. To help you gear up for this work, think through the following questions. If a passionate prayer life is your goal, you'll need to put some serious thought into your answers.

1. What are the most important qualities of a healthy, growing prayer life? What makes them so important?

2. What's good and what's bad about the way you pray right now?

3. How hard would it be for you to change the way you pray? Why? What do you think would be the most difficult thing for you to change? Why?

4. On a scale of one to ten (with one being pathetic and ten being amazing), how creative is your prayer life right now? On a scale of one to ten, how unique is your prayer life right now? On a scale of one to ten, how persistent is your prayer life right now? On a scale of one to ten, how frequently do you pray?

5. What changes could make your prayer life more creative?

6. What changes could make your prayer life more unique or personalized?

7. What changes could make your prayers more persistent?

8. What changes could you make to your schedule that would allow you to pray more frequently?

one from the heart

Based on what you've learned about prayer and what you've read of the psalmists' prayers in this chapter, write your own prayer to God. Be sure to incorporate as much creativity, uniqueness, and persistence as you can into your prayer.

4

CREDIT WHERE CREDIT'S DUE

"Kobe! Kobe!"

Kobe Bryant turned and saw a teenage guy in a Lakers jersey sprinting across the airport terminal toward him.

"I can't believe it's you!" the breathless young man said. "You're my idol! I've taped every game you've ever played."

"Well, that's nice to hear," Kobe said with a smile. "Hey, man, my plane doesn't leave for another hour. Want to sit down and chill for a while? We can talk about ball or anything else you want."

The young man stared at him in amazement. "You and me— talking?" he asked.

"Yeah," Kobe said casually as he plopped down in a seat, "I like getting to know people. We'll talk about anything you want."

"Awesome, let's talk about some of those mind-blowing things you do on the court."

"Like what?" Kobe asked.

"Well, a couple of years ago you were playing Sacramento," the young man said, "and in the third quarter, you shot a free throw that just barely touched the rim as it went in. I've never forgotten that."

"Huh? A free throw?" Kobe asked in surprise. "That's all you want to talk about?"

"No, there's more," the young man said. "There was a game last year against the Pacers that was just incredible. At halftime, you dribbled a ball all the way from your bench to the locker room. It must have been at least fifty feet. I couldn't believe what I was seeing!"

"That's it?" Kobe asked, disappointed. "Of all the things in the world you could have talked to me about, you pick those two? Have you ever seen anything else I've done?"

it's like this

How lame would it be to get a chance to talk to a superstar and then blow it by bringing up all kinds of insignificant things? But that's what happens in prayer all the time. Every time we pray, we have an opportunity to praise God in a one-on-one setting. And what happens? Often, if we praise Him at all, it's for small favors He's done for us—things that, in the grand scheme of things, are about as significant as Kobe Bryant hitting a free throw.

Don't misunderstand. There's nothing wrong with praising God for little things as long as you don't overlook the big things in the process.

You'll also need to be careful not to praise God for the wrong reasons. There's a temptation to use praise as a way of buttering up God before asking Him for things in prayer. It's the same method you've probably used on a boss or teacher at one time or another. ("Have you lost weight? You look really good. By the way, I need Friday off.")

With God, the flattery process usually goes more like this: "O Lord, You are all-powerful and all-knowing, full of grace and love. And that's why I'm turning to You now, asking You to give us good weather in Florida next week during our vacation." Of course, not all insincere efforts to praise God are that awkward. But they're all obvious to Him. It's tough to fake sincerity when the One you're talking to can read your mind.

God knows when you're being genuine and honest with Him and when you're blowing smoke just to get something you want. So if you're not coming to God with sincere praise that comes from the bottom of your heart, you might as well not even bother praising Him at all.

And then you can kiss your chances for an extreme prayer life good-bye. You see, if praising God is not one of the main reasons that you pray, you can't really claim to have a legitimate prayer life. Without praise, prayer becomes a self-centered activity. Instead of focusing outward on God, you start to focus inward on your situation and requests.

And nothing good can come from that.

So if you're serious about wanting to experience extreme prayer, you've got to know how to give God extreme praise. And if you've read the first three chapters of this book, you know where we're going for examples of how to praise God. That's right—straight to the book of Psalms.

Word

The psalmists were passionate about praising God. They took praise to a whole new level. Those guys were constantly searching for new ways to express how they felt about God and His works. In their prayers, they focused on three specific areas of praise that we can use as starting points for our prayers. The psalmists praised God for the following:

1. Who He is
2. What He's done
3. What He's doing

Let's explore each of these areas to see if we can pick up some important tips.

I. praising god for who he is

In Chapter 2, we talked about the importance of getting to know the One you're praying to. But simply knowing who God is isn't enough. If you're serious about taking your prayer life to the limit, then you've got to find ways to tell God how you feel about Him. You've got to tell Him what it is about Him that amazes you, excites you, makes you thankful, and blows your mind.

David certainly wasn't shy when it came to sharing his feelings about the Lord:

Bless the LORD, O my soul;
And all that is within me, bless His holy name!
Bless the LORD, O my soul,

And forget not all His benefits:

Who forgives all your iniquities,

Who heals all your diseases,

Who redeems your life from destruction,

Who crowns you with lovingkindness and tender mercies,

Who satisfies your mouth with good things,

So that your youth is renewed like the eagle's.

The LORD executes righteousness

And justice for all who are oppressed.

He made known His ways to Moses,

His acts to the children of Israel.

The LORD is merciful and gracious,

Slow to anger, and abounding in mercy.

He will not always strive with us,

Nor will He keep His anger forever.

He has not dealt with us according to our sins,

Nor punished us according to our iniquities.

For as the heavens are high above the earth,

So great is His mercy toward those who fear Him;

As far as the east is from the west,

So far has He removed our transgressions from us.

As a father pities his children,

So the LORD pities those who fear Him.

For He knows our frame;

He remembers that we are dust.

As for man, his days are like grass;

As a flower of the field, so he flourishes.

For the wind passes over it, and it is gone,

And its place remembers it no more.

But the mercy of the LORD is from everlasting to everlasting

On those who fear Him,

And His righteousness to children's children,

To such as keep His covenant,

And to those who remember His commandments to do them.

The LORD has established His throne in heaven,

And His kingdom rules over all.

Bless the LORD, you His angels,

Who excel in strength, who do His word,

Heeding the voice of His word.

Bless the LORD, all you His hosts,

You ministers of His, who do His pleasure.

Bless the LORD, all His works,

In all places of His dominion.

Bless the LORD, O my soul! (Ps. 103)

From this psalm, we see that God's forgiveness, healing power, justice, and compassion for the needy were pretty important and impressive to David. Notice the way he described God's mercy when it comes to our sin: "As far as the east is from the west, so far has He removed our transgressions from us."

And to get across the idea of God's eternal nature, David made a creative comparison: "As for man, his days are like grass . . . But the mercy of the LORD is from everlasting to everlasting." In the space of twenty-two verses, David managed to squeeze in references to almost a dozen of God's attributes. In other psalms, he chose to single out one or two attributes and focus his entire prayer on them. (There are no minimum requirements when it comes to praising God.)

If you want to improve your praise beyond the "God,

You're really awesome" level, then you've got to expand your view of Him. And there's really only one way to do that. You've got to jam your nose in the pages of your Bible and explore the passages that mention God to see if you can pick up some clues about His nature and attributes.

To get you started, check out this list of attributes that will probably sound familiar to some degree. Each attribute could supply you with enough material for a year's worth of prayers if you're willing to study them and think about what they really mean to you. Some of the big words might make your eyes glaze over, but they're just impressive terms for simple thoughts.

Praise God for these attributes:

- His compassion—the fact that He has a special place in His heart for poor, needy, and hurting people
- His eternal nature—the fact that He has no beginning and no end
- His grace—the fact that He treats us way better than we deserve to be treated
- His holiness—the fact that there is no trace of sin found anywhere near Him
- His immanence—the fact that He is willing to get involved personally with His creation
- His omnipotence—the fact that He is able to do anything at any time
- His omnipresence—the fact that nothing escapes His attention because He is everywhere at the same time
- His omniscience—the fact that He knows everything, from our most heartfelt desires to our most private hurts

Keep in mind that simply mentioning these attributes to God in prayer is not praise. Praising God involves making

> praising god involves making his attributes personal.

His attributes personal. When you say, "God, You are gracious," all you're doing is stating the obvious. What does His grace mean to you? When have you experienced it in the past? What would your life be like if you hadn't experienced it?

These are just some of the questions you'll need to wrestle with as you search for ways to praise God.

2. praising god for what he's done

While you're in the Bible searching for clues about who God is, keep an eye out for examples of what He's done. The Bible is a record of God's work on behalf of His people. Some of the stories of His work are action-packed; others are more subdued. Some are flat-out miraculous; others are more ordinary. Yet all of them are amazing for one reason: they're evidence of the fact that God has done—and will continue to do—whatever it takes to bring people to Him.

If you're going to praise God for what He's done, then there's no better place to start with than creation. Check out how the author of Psalm 104 incorporated praise for God's creation into his prayer:

> Bless the LORD, O my soul!
> O LORD my God, You are very great:
> You are clothed with honor and majesty,

Who cover Yourself with light as with a garment,
Who stretch out the heavens like a curtain.
He lays the beams of His upper chambers in the waters,
Who makes the clouds His chariot,
Who walks on the wings of the wind,
Who makes His angels spirits,
His ministers a flame of fire.
You who laid the foundations of the earth,
So that it should not be moved forever,
You covered it with the deep as with a garment;
The waters stood above the mountains.
At Your rebuke they fled;
At the voice of Your thunder they hastened away.
They went up over the mountains;
They went down into the valleys,
To the place which You founded for them.
You have set a boundary that they may not pass over,
That they may not return to cover the earth.
He sends the springs into the valleys;
They flow among the hills.
They give drink to every beast of the field;
The wild donkeys quench their thirst.
By them the birds of the heavens have their home;
They sing among the branches.
He waters the hills from His upper chambers;
The earth is satisfied with the fruit of Your works.
He causes the grass to grow for the cattle,
And vegetation for the service of man,
That he may bring forth food from the earth,
And wine that makes glad the heart of man,

Oil to make his face shine,
And bread which strengthens man's heart.
The trees of the LORD are full of sap,
The cedars of Lebanon which He planted,
Where the birds make their nests;
The stork has her home in the fir trees.
The high hills are for the wild goats;
The cliffs are a refuge for the rock badgers.
He appointed the moon for seasons;
The sun knows its going down.
You make darkness, and it is night,
In which all the beasts of the forest creep about.
The young lions roar after their prey,
And seek their food from God.
When the sun rises, they gather together
And lie down in their dens.
Man goes out to his work
And to his labor until the evening.
O LORD, how manifold are Your works!
In wisdom You have made them all.
The earth is full of Your possessions—
This great and wide sea,
In which are innumerable teeming things,
Living things both small and great.
There the ships sail about;
There is that Leviathan
Which You have made to play there.
These all wait for You,
That You may give them their food in due season.
What You give them they gather in;

You open Your hand, they are filled with good.

You hide Your face, they are troubled;

You take away their breath, they die and return to their dust.

You send forth Your Spirit, they are created;

And You renew the face of the earth.

May the glory of the LORD endure forever;

May the LORD rejoice in His works.

He looks on the earth, and it trembles;

He touches the hills, and they smoke.

I will sing to the LORD as long as I live;

I will sing praise to my God while I have my being.

May my meditation be sweet to Him;

I will be glad in the LORD.

May sinners be consumed from the earth,

And the wicked be no more.

Bless the LORD, O my soul!

Praise the LORD! (Ps. 104)

In the psalmist's description of God's creative work he was doing more than saying, "Lord, You create pretty sunsets." He was connecting the dots between different areas of creation to show just how perfect the Lord's design of nature is. Springs provide water for animals and people alike. Fir trees provide a home for storks. Mountain cliffs provide a home for rock badgers. Everything has a purpose.

These aren't observations that just occurred to someone one day. The psalmist must have spent a good chunk of time studying the natural world around him and applying what he found to what he knew of God. The result was that he was able to bring an incredible form of praise to God.

You can do the same thing, even if you're not the out-doorsy type. All it takes is an awareness of the world around you and a God-centered perspective. Put it this way: if you're constantly looking for reasons to praise God, then you'll find them.

And creation is just the beginning (literally) of what God has done. Every book in the Bible contains stories of His work. Many books contain hundreds of stories. You can build an entire prayer's worth of praise around any of them. The more you know about those stories, the better equipped you'll be to offer heartfelt praise for them. So do I really need to tell you that the Bible is your most important tool for building an extreme prayer life?

The fact that we even have the Bible is another reason to praise God. (Notice how, once you get started looking for reasons to praise God, you find them everywhere.) God could have chosen to remain a mystery to us. But He gave us His Word to tell us everything we need to know about Him, His work, and His will. How much praise would you say He deserves for that?

> if you're constantly looking for reasons to praise God, then you'll find them.

Of everything God has done, though, there's one thing that deserves our praise 24/7. That's the sacrifice He made to give us the hope of spending eternity with Him. Remember, by God's standards, we're all slimeballs. He's holy, which means He can't have anything to do with sin. He's also perfectly just, which means He must punish sin with what it deserves, which is death.

Unfortunately for us, from the time we're born, we're covered with sin. We reek of it. And though we must seem disgusting to God, He loves us. In fact, He loves us so much that He decided to send Someone to take the punishment for our sin. The problem was that only a perfect person, someone without sin, could do it.

And the only person whose résumé fit the job was Jesus, God's only Son.

So God sent His Son to earth as a human being, knowing that He would be mocked, laughed at, rejected, betrayed, beaten, tortured, and murdered. How horrible do you think it must have been for God to let Jesus go, knowing what was in store for Him? How excruciating do you think it was for Him to watch the people He was trying to save viciously kill His Son?

How can you praise God enough for making that kind of sacrifice for you?

→ **HEADS UP**

Psalms 105, 106, and 107 praise God for His work. During the early years of Israel's history, people like Abraham, Isaac, Jacob, and Moses seemed to have one dramatic encounter with God after another. Every time they turned around He was making covenants with them, rescuing someone, punishing the people of Israel, or performing miracles for them.

In these prayers, the psalmist was saying, "Lord, those things may have happened a long time ago, but You still deserve praise for them." The psalmist went into quite a bit of detail:

He sent a man before them—
Joseph—who was sold as a slave.
They hurt his feet with fetters,
He was laid in irons.
Until the time that his word came to pass,
The word of the LORD tested him.
The king sent and released him,
The ruler of the people let him go free. (Ps. 105:17–20)

Is there any doubt that the psalmist knew what he was talking about?

You might consider using these psalms as models when you praise God for His work in biblical times. Just be sure to get your facts straight so that you can go into as much detail as possible. Remember, specific praise is the best kind.

3. praising god for what he's doing

Of course, it's not as though God retired when the Bible was finished. Every day He continues to do more praise-worthy things than we could count in a lifetime:

Through the LORD's mercies we are not consumed,
Because His compassions fail not.
They are new every morning;
Great is Your faithfulness. (Lam. 3:22–23)

"New every morning"—sounds as if it belongs in a commercial for milk or bread, doesn't it? Guaranteed freshness.

Think of the Lamentations passage as a commercial for God. We never have to worry about a shortage of things to praise God for because He ships in a whole new truckload every morning for us to discover and think about. Our supply is endless—as long as we're paying attention, that is.

David certainly paid attention to God's work in his life. And as a result, he came up with one of the most famous examples of praise ever written:

The LORD is my shepherd;
I shall not want.
He makes me to lie down in green pastures;
He leads me beside the still waters.
He restores my soul;
He leads me in the paths of righteousness
For His name's sake.
Yea, though I walk through the valley
    of the shadow of death,
I will fear no evil;
For You are with me;
Your rod and Your staff, they comfort me.
You prepare a table before me
    in the presence of my enemies;
You anoint my head with oil;
My cup runs over.
Surely goodness and mercy shall follow me
All the days of my life;
And I will dwell in the house of the LORD
Forever. (Ps. 23)

In just six short verses, David managed to give up praise for:

- the way God provided for him ("I shall not want").
- the way God helped him get his head together ("He leads me beside the still waters").
- the way God kept him safe in dangerous situations ("I will fear no evil").
- the way God guaranteed his future ("I will dwell in the house of the LORD forever").

What's especially cool about this psalm is the way David added a personal touch to each of his praises. He didn't just say, "God, You are a great provider and protector." He said, "[Because of You] I shall not want," and "I will fear no evil; for You are with me." David wasn't just praising God for things he'd read about; he was praising God for things he'd experienced firsthand. In case you're wondering, that's extreme praise.

What's it to You?

How's this for a weird concept? Praising God actually does more for you than it does for Him. Keep in mind that God is perfect and that He knows He's perfect. He doesn't need compliments from you to feel good about Himself. He doesn't have self-image problems. He doesn't need an ego boost.

Praising God gives you a chance to show the Lord, yourself, and the people around you that you "get it." It's really simple. Either you recognize and appreciate what God does in your life and in the world, or you don't. If you recognize it, then you gain a whole new understanding of the world around you. You see things more clearly. The *whys* and *hows* of everyday life make more sense to you.

If you don't recognize it, or if it's no big deal to you, you've got no shot at becoming an extreme pray-er.

one last thing

Before I wrap up this chapter, I need to clear up a potential misunderstanding. Throughout the chapter, I've mentioned things such as spending time in the Bible and studying nature as ways to prepare yourself to praise God. However, I don't want to give you the impression that there should always be a little work involved when you praise God.

Actually there should be a *lot* of work involved.

Praising God isn't an assignment to blow off or take lightly. Whatever you do, don't come to Him with praise that you haven't thought out carefully. Meaningless praise is worse than no praise at all because it turns your prayer time into something fake. And God doesn't do fake.

taking it to heart

Time to put the ol' gray matter to work. Learning how to praise God sincerely is going to take some work. Are you ready for it? To get you in shape for the job that lies ahead, think through the following questions. If an extreme prayer life is your goal, then get ready to work through these ideas.

1. How do you think God responds to praise? Do you think it has any effect on Him?

2. What kinds of things have you praised God for in the past? How sincere would you say you were in your praise?

3. Of all the Bible stories you know about God, which ones really make you want to praise Him? Why are those stories so meaningful to you?

4. Which of God's attributes or characteristics is most important to you right now? Why?

5. Which of God's attributes or characteristics is most mysterious or confusing to you right now? Why?

6. Write down three things you can do this week to sharpen your skills when it comes to praising God. Be specific.

One from the heart

Based on what you've learned about praising God and what you've read of the psalmists' prayers in this chapter, write your own prayer to God. Be sure to share your thoughts and feelings about who He is and what He's done. And try to be as specific as possible throughout your prayer.

5

THANK YOU, THANK YOU VERY MUCH

When I was in fourth grade, my father made the decision to leave the small rural church he pastored in order to go back to school. For my younger sisters and me, that meant leaving the home and church we'd grown up in and moving to a new state. Our close friends in the congregation knew how much we were dreading the move and did their best to comfort us.

Mabel, an elderly widow in the church, did more than just try to comfort us, though. She asked us kids to give her a list of our favorite foods so that she could prepare a special dinner for us the day before we moved.

Now what kids could restrain themselves with an offer like that on the table? Certainly not us! We let our imaginations (and greed) run wild and came up with a list that looked more like a novel. Every kind of junk food you can imagine—ice-cream sundaes, fried chicken, barbecue potato chips, hamburgers, five kinds of soda—was on that list. We figured the more we asked for, the better chance we stood of having at least one or two of our requests honored.

It turns out that we had seriously underestimated Mabel. When we got to her house, we found everything we had requested. Everything. And it was no small list, either. Who knows how much money she spent to make our dinner special.

My sisters and I tried to eat as much of it as we could, but it turned out that our desires were bigger than our stomachs. More than half of the food that Mabel prepared went untouched. But Mabel didn't seem to mind. She put the leftovers into three big ol' grocery bags for us to take with us.

When it was time to leave, my sisters and I got into our usual argument about which of us would get to sit in the back of the station wagon on the way home. It didn't matter that we were in someone else's house or that we'd just been served the meal of our lives or that our parents were doing everything they could to calmly stop us from arguing. The fight was on, and we weren't going to stop until one of us got his or her way. At some point, Mabel tried to say good-bye to us, but we were too busy arguing to respond.

Finally Mom had had enough. She wanted us out of Mabel's house ASAP so that she could give us an earful. "What do you say to Mabel for the nice meal she made for you?" Mom asked through gritted teeth.

"Thanks," I mumbled without even bothering to look at Mabel. Just the kind of response you'd expect from a jerky nine-year-old. My parents made embarrassed apologies for the way we were acting as they pushed us out the door, and we all left.

As childhood stories go, this one isn't what you'd call a spell-binder. Heck, I probably would have forgotten it if it hadn't been

for one thing. As I was being pushed out the door that day, I hap-
pened to glance back at Mabel. We made eye contact for less than
a second, but that was enough for me to see the disappointment,
anger, and hurt she was feeling. And I knew that I had caused her
to feel that way.

One heartfelt "thank you" and maybe a few extra-nice com-
ments would have made Mabel's day. But I was too wrapped up
in trying to get the next thing I wanted to think about that. So I
took her kindness, generosity, and love for granted. Maybe I was
even enough of a jerk as a nine-year-old to believe that I deserved
what she did for me.

Whatever the reason, my lack of response stung Mabel. That
was obvious from the look on her face. Maybe it even broke her
heart. I don't know—I never saw her again. She died years later
when I was in college. I still think about that day at her house some-
times. And when I do, I always go back to that one moment when I
had the chance to show Mabel the gratitude she deserved—to give
a little back to her after she'd given so much to me—but choked.

it's like this

Time for a little perspective. The meal that Mabel made
for my family and me was an incredible example of generosity and love. But it was just one meal. Compare that to what
God does for us every day, and you'll get an idea of just how
much gratitude we owe Him.

Want to get specific? Let's do it.

Do you have a place to live? A family that loves you?
Friends who care about you? How about an education? Do
you have access to water and food whenever you need them?

Do you have your sight? What about your hearing? Do your arms and legs work okay? Are you generally healthy? Do you live in a safe neighborhood? Can you worship God freely, without worrying about being arrested or killed? Do you have enough clothes to keep you warm? Do you have any talents, skills, or abilities? Do you have access to transportation to get you where you need to go? Do you have the mental ability to understand what you're reading? Have you ever noticed the beauty of the world around you? Do you have any leisure time? How about a job that allows you to support yourself or your family? Do you like your church? Is your life sweet for the most part? Does your future look bright? Do you believe you'll go to heaven when you die?

If you answered yes to any of these questions, you have a lot to be thankful for. If you answered yes to most of them, you may not realize how blessed you really are. And that's a major problemo.

You see, if you don't have a clue about what you've been given, then you don't have much to talk to God about. You may think you do, but you don't. Remember, one-sided prayer really isn't prayer at all. If you're loading God up with new requests all the time and not giving Him the praise He deserves when He comes through for you, then you can't really claim to have a tight relationship with Him.

You'd be disrespecting God in the same way I disrespected Mabel years ago—only you'd be doing it day after day after day. And you don't have to be a Bible scholar to know that disrespecting God is a bad idea.

Sometimes, as an excuse, people try to use God's omniscience (the fact that He knows everything) against Him.

They say, "God already knows I'm thankful for everything He does for me. I don't need to tell Him."

How lame is that?

It's like saying, "My parents know I care about them; it's okay if I treat them like dirt," or, "My boyfriend already knows I love him; I don't need to spend any time with him." Bottom line—it's just plain rude.

Worse than that, though, it's also a sign of a screwed-up prayer life. If you regard giving thanks to God as a minor part of your communication with Him, or as something you can skip when time is running short, then you need to flip your priorities around . . . oh, about 180 degrees.

Being thankful isn't just about making God feel good. God's not going to throw a fit or start pouting because you forget to say thank You for something. This is about getting your head straight. Either you're the type of person who recognizes and appreciates what God does for you, or you're the type who takes Him for granted.

Guess which type is more likely to become an extreme pray-er?

Word

The psalmists knew how to give God His props. When the Lord did something for them, they were all over it with gratitude and appreciation. And it wasn't just, "Thanks, God. That was a cool thing to do." No, the psalmists went on for paragraphs about how God's actions had made a difference in their lives. They didn't just want to say, "Thanks." They wanted to make God look good in the process.

Psalm 116 is a good example of how seriously the psalmists took thanksgiving. Check out the details the author tossed in as he tried to express his gratefulness for what God had done:

I love the LORD, because He has heard
My voice and my supplications.
Because He has inclined His ear to me,
Therefore I will call upon Him as long as I live.
The pains of death surrounded me,
And the pangs of Sheol laid hold of me;
I found trouble and sorrow.
Then I called upon the name of the LORD:
"O LORD, I implore You, deliver my soul!"
Gracious is the LORD, and righteous;
Yes, our God is merciful.
The LORD preserves the simple;
I was brought low, and He saved me.
Return to your rest, O my soul,
For the LORD has dealt bountifully with you.
For You have delivered my soul from death,
My eyes from tears,
And my feet from falling.
I will walk before the LORD
In the land of the living.
I believed, therefore I spoke,
"I am greatly afflicted."
I said in my haste,
"All men are liars."
What shall I render to the LORD
For all His benefits toward me?

I will take up the cup of salvation,
And call upon the name of the LORD.
I will pay my vows to the LORD
Now in the presence of all His people.
Precious in the sight of the LORD
Is the death of His saints.
O LORD, truly I am Your servant;
I am Your servant, the son of Your maidservant;
You have loosed my bonds.
I will offer to You the sacrifice of thanksgiving,
And will call upon the name of the LORD.
I will pay my vows to the LORD
Now in the presence of all His people,
In the courts of the LORD's house,
In the midst of you, O Jerusalem.
Praise the LORD!

Based on the clues scattered throughout this prayer, the psalmist had reason to be thankful. People don't write, "The pains of death surrounded me," and, "I am greatly afflicted," unless they're in serious trouble. Apparently the psalmist had been staring death in the face. Maybe he was injured, or maybe he was just sick. Either way, he must have been in bad physical shape.

The only thing he knew to do was to turn to God for help. Look at his words again: "I implore You." This guy was begging the Lord not to let him die.

And what did God do? In the psalmist's words, "He saved me," and He "delivered my soul from death." As answers to prayer go, you can't get much better than that one.

So the psalmist prayed, and the Lord answered. For some people, that would have been the end of the story. But not for the psalmist. There was still one more thing he had to do: "I will pay my vows to the LORD."

Vows were serious business in ancient Israel. They were like unwritten contracts. If you made one, you were expected to keep it, no matter what. From the psalmist's point of view, giving thanks in prayer was like keeping a vow. If you didn't do it, you were breaking a legal agreement.

The psalmist wasn't just being polite ("Say thank You to the nice deity, Davey"); he was fulfilling his part of the contract. His prayer of gratitude was not just a way of saying thank You but also a way of paying tribute to the Lord. God had honored him by answering his prayer; the psalmist honored God by making a big deal of it.

> halfhearted thanks have no place in extreme prayer.

When God answers your prayers, He's entitled to your gratitude. It's that simple. If you don't give Him your gratitude, you're sabotaging your prayer life. Halfhearted thanks have no place in extreme prayer. If you're not willing to kick it up a notch when it comes to showing your appreciation to the Lord, you'll never discover what prayer is all about.

→ **HEADS UP**

Luke 17:11–19 tells the story of ten men with leprosy who caught Jesus' attention while He was walking through

Samaria one day. "Jesus, Master, have mercy on us!" they shouted.

A quick word of explanation here: leprosy was a nasty disease in more ways than one. In serious cases, a person's skin would literally rot away. It wasn't unusual for people with leprosy to lose fingers, toes, hands, feet—even arms and legs. In addition to physical suffering, the people with the disease had to deal with rejection. The ancient Israelites were big on cleanliness. They rejected anything they considered unclean. Even a mild case of leprosy was enough to make you an outcast in Jewish society.

Maybe the ten men with leprosy in Samaria had heard stories of Jesus' healing power. Or maybe they just recognized something in Him that made them think He could help them. Whatever the reason, the men must have been desperate as they yelled to Jesus for help.

Their desperation paid off. With one simple sentence, "Go, show yourselves to the priests," Jesus healed all ten men. The disease that had ruined their lives was gone forever. Can you imagine how they must have felt when they saw that the oozing sores on their body had cleared up? Can you imagine how they must have felt when they realized they could become part of normal society again? Can you imagine how thankful they must have been?

Actually you have to imagine it because the Bible suggests that nine of the ten men never thought twice about Jesus or His miracle. They took off to see the priests and kept right on going. They had a new life but didn't seem to care how they'd gotten it.

Only one of the men who had been healed felt the need to thank Jesus for what He'd done. Among other things, he praised God as loudly as he could, fell on his face at Jesus' feet, and let Him know just how glad he was to be healthy again. In other words, he showed extreme gratitude.

The other nine blew off the miracle as if it had never happened and moved on to the next thing. Their attitudes were totally self-centered, not God-centered.

If that seems incredibly rude and outrageous, consider the things you've forgotten to thank the Lord for in your life.

What's it to You?

The quest to be totally thankful in prayer is nothing new. Check out these historic prayers:

> Thou hast given so much to me,
> Give one more thing—a grateful heart;
> Not thankful when it pleases me,
> As if thy blessings had spare days;
> But such a heart whose very pulse may be
> Thy praise. (George Herbert, 1593–1633)

O God, we thank you for this earth, our home; for the wide sky and the blessed sun, for the salt sea and the running water, for the everlasting hills and the never-resting winds, for trees and the common grass underfoot.

We thank you for our senses by which we hear the songs of birds, and see the splendors of the summer fields, and taste of the autumn fruits, and rejoice in the feel of the snow, and smell the breath of the spring.

Grant us a heart wide open to all this beauty; and save our souls from being so blind that we pass unseeing when even the common thornbush is aflame with your glory, O God our creator, who lives and reigns for ever and ever. (Walter Rauschenbusch, 1861–1918)

Look at those dates next to George Herbert's name. He lived four hundred years ago and struggled with the same gratitude problems we face today. He knew he needed something more than convenient thankfulness, being grateful only when it pleased him. He wanted a heart full of gratefulness.

Walter Rauschenbusch, on the other hand, wanted to be more aware of everything he had to be grateful for. He knew that everything in creation—even the thornbush—showed that God deserves our praise. He wanted to be able to see it.

Praying for a grateful spirit (as George and Walter did) is one way to pump up your thankfulness. Here are a couple of additional suggestions.

feel it before you say it

Saying thanks isn't hard. You do it all the time. When a guy behind the counter at McDonald's hands you a Quarter Pounder, you say, "Thanks." When someone says he likes your shirt, you say, "Thanks." When someone stops to help you fix a flat tire, you say, "Thanks."

Maybe you're really thankful when you say it, or maybe

you're just trying to be polite. Either way, it's cool. No one's going to question your motives for thanking him. No one except God, that is. When it comes to being thankful to God, either your feelings come from your heart, or they don't. And if they don't, then don't bother trying to fake it. God knows.

Earlier in the chapter, I tossed out a bunch of questions to get you thinking about what you have to be thankful for. If you're not sure that your thankfulness is coming from your heart, try asking, "What if?"

- What if you'd been born in East Africa and had to worry about starving to death?
- What if you lived in a neighborhood run by gangbangers and had to worry about getting jumped or shot every time you walked out the door?
- What if you suddenly lost your home and had to live on the streets?

When you think about what *could be,* it tends to make you appreciate what *is.* And once you start to feel that appreciation, you can tell God all about it.

Being thankful is more than just saying thanks. It's also a way of admitting that you depend on God for the good things in your life. It's a way of recognizing that without God's help, life would be a serious drag.

count your blessings—literally

You live in a busy world. Every day you have dozens of conversations, assignments, and requests to keep track of.

Throw in the hundreds of messages you get daily from the TV, radio, and Net, and you've got a horde of information scrambling for a prime spot in your memory. The more people and images you encounter, the more difficult it becomes to remember them all.

This information overload explains why, if you're not careful, you can lose track of what God has done in your life. The details of His work tend to get swept away when the next wave of info comes crashing in.

If you are careful, on the other hand, you'll find a way to anchor that information so that it doesn't get lost. That's where a prayer journal comes in handy. When you pray for something, make a habit of writing down the request and putting the date next to it. When God answers your prayer, do the same. That way, you'll not only have documented proof of God's work in your life (which may come in handy the next time you're feeling down or abandoned), but you'll also have a cheat sheet for your prayers of thanksgiving. When it comes time to share your gratitude with God, you'll have mini "cue cards" to remind you.

Keep in mind, though, that some of God's answers to prayer are more obvious than others. If you want a complete prayer journal, you're going to have to learn to recognize and appreciate even the small things that God does for you. It will take some work at first. Until you discover the many areas of your life where God's answers to prayer can be found, you may become discouraged in your search.

Don't give up, though. With a little practice, you'll get the hang of it. Once you get used to looking for answered prayers, you'll see them everywhere.

make sure your actions match your words

Some of the psalms were public property for worship services, but some of them were extremely personal. Remember Psalm 51? It's like a page out of David's journal. He let it all hang out in that psalm, and he didn't even try to make himself look good. The psalmists weren't just showing off by writing fancy psalms for a church service. Often, the psalms were just between them and God, and they were written from the heart.

It wasn't enough for the psalmists to say, "Thank You, God, for all You've done for me." No, they made a big deal of it. If you read between the lines of many psalms, one of the emotions you'll find is amazement. The attitude that comes across is, "Can you believe the almighty Creator of the universe is paying attention to somebody like me?"

And that's a great attitude to have because everyone can relate to it. If you, a normal person, have the guts to start telling others what the almighty Creator is doing in your life—how He listens to and answers your prayers—you'll find that people respond in amazing ways. If you don't think you're the type of person God can use to change lives, think again.

one last thing

Keep one other thing in mind as you're bouncing around this idea of thankfulness. Someone has to get credit for the good things that happen in your life. Usually what happens is that if God doesn't get it, well, then, you do. When people who don't know you well see the blessings in your life, they may assume that you're something special or that you've done all right for yourself. If you don't do anything to change that impression, then it's like taking credit for God's work.

Do you really want to take anything, including credit, from God?

The apostle Paul, talking about salvation, summed things up this way: "For by grace you have been saved through faith, and that not of yourselves; it is the gift of God, not of works, lest anyone should boast" (Eph. 2:8–9).

The same thing holds true for every area of your life.

taking it to heart

Time to put the ol' gray matter to work. Developing a thankful spirit is going to require some time and practice. To help you prepare, work through the following questions. If a passionate prayer life is your goal, you'll need to put some serious thought into your answers.

1. What is the most amazing thing God has ever done for you? How did you respond?
2. Write down three things that, until now, you've forgotten to thank God for. How do you feel about your forgetfulness in these areas? How do you think God feels?
3. Why does God want us to maintain thankful hearts?
4. How do you react when people forget to say thank you to you? How do you think your reaction differs from God's reaction when His answers to prayer go unmentioned?
5. What can you do to make sure that your gratefulness comes from your heart?
6. Write down three things, other than praying, that you can

do this week to start developing a more thankful attitude toward God.

7. What changes are you going to make to your prayer life
in order to give God the credit He deserves?

One from the heart

Based on what you've learned about thankfulness and
what you've read of the prayers in this chapter, write your
own prayer to God. Be sure to share your thoughts and feelings about what He's done in your life. And try to be as specific as possible throughout your prayer.

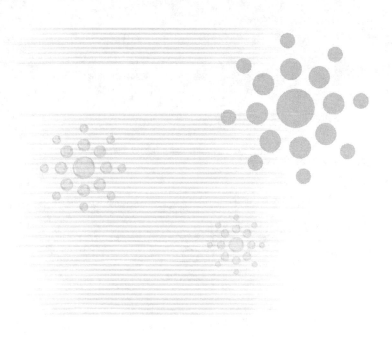

6

PRAYING FOR ANOTHER

My sister was always one of those hard-core, straight-A students before she started hanging around with a bunch of stoners. I don't know why she dumped her old friends, but as soon as she did, her grades dropped. My parents started freaking out, but they didn't know what to do. They tried to ground her, but she just ignored them. Dad threatened to kick her out of the house, but she just said she'd go live with one of her friends. That really scared my parents. One day when I came home from school, Dad and Mom were sitting on the couch. They both had bloodshot eyes, like they'd been crying. I figured someone had died, but they just said they'd been talking about my sister. Then they asked me to pray for her with them. What could I say? We all kneeled in the middle of the living room and held hands. It felt kind of weird but at the same time so relieving, too, if you know what I mean. I asked God to take care of my sister. My dad asked Him to help her realize that she was ruining her life. The next weekend, my sister was at a party that got raided. The police didn't arrest her because she didn't have any drugs on her. But they did make her call my dad to come pick her up at the police station. Dad said he'd never seen her so scared. The next morning, she came downstairs with a pile of posters and CD's and said she'd decided not to party anymore.

—Matt, age fourteen

❋　　❋　　❋

A guy in my youth group was in a coma after a car wreck. He had massive head injuries. The doctors said there was no hope for recovery. They said if he lived, he'd pretty much be a vegetable. They said there was no chance he'd ever walk again. At first, we all felt so hopeless. But then someone in the group said, "Why don't we pray for him?" So we started this prayer chain where one person would be praying for him at all times. We had a schedule worked out and everything. The whole group really got into it. About three days after we started praying, he came out of his coma. We were going to stop praying then, but we decided to keep going. A few days after that, he took his first steps. Now the doctors say there's a chance he might recover 100 percent. They can't believe it. They just keep saying the brain responds in mysterious ways. We say it's God who responds in mysterious ways.

—Lindsay, age seventeen

❋　　❋　　❋

My dad and his father never had what you'd call a close relationship. My grandfather was a stubborn, critical, bitter man *who never showed his kids much love or affection. The older my grandfather got, the harder my dad tried to make some kind of a connection with him. But it seemed like the more my dad tried to work things out, the more my grandfather shot him down. It always killed me to see my dad rejected by his own father. I used to pray that God would change my grandfather's heart, but I couldn't imagine how He would do it. Then one day we got the call Dad had been dreading. My grandfather had had a stroke that left him unable to walk or speak. The first time my dad and I went to see him in the hospital, though, we discovered that the stroke had had one other effect on him, as well. When we walked in the room, my grandfather grinned and waved us over to the bed with his one good arm. He couldn't form any words, but there was no mistaking the sounds he was making. He was happy, almost giddy, to see us. When my dad got to the bed, my grandfather reached out, grabbed his hand and started squeezing it. That simple gesture was almost too much for my dad to take. Tears welled up in his eyes. He started to ask my grandfather how he was feeling but got all choked up. So we just sat there in silence, watching the joy in both of their eyes, while my grandfather squeezed my dad's hand.*

—Eddie, age twenty-three

it's like this

Have you ever seen someone's life changed by prayer? We're talking about an obvious, no-doubt-about-it, only-God-could-have-done-that change in someone's life. We're talking about the kind of answer to prayer that sends a shiver up your spine and makes you think, *Whoa.* The kind that smacks down conventional wisdom and forces so-called experts to say,

- "There is no medical explanation for his recovery."
- "The situation has improved dramatically."
- "We're not sure what triggered the change in her behavior."
- "His development has far exceeded all expectations."

If you've ever seen . . .

- an addict get clean or an alcoholic get sober,
- a person with cancer go into remission,
- an accident victim recover from devastating injuries,
- an unbeliever accept Christ,
- a couple experience the wife's pregnancy after years of trying,
- a family reunited after years of bitterness and separation,

. . . and known that people were praying for it, then you know what a mind-blowing experience it is to see God at work.

Here's the thing. Deep down we all know that prayer works. The Bible says so, other Christians say so, and the Holy Spirit's voice inside us says so. If it didn't work, you wouldn't be doing it, and I wouldn't be writing about it. But when you get a glimpse of one of those "neon light" answers to prayer, the kind that's obvious enough for even non-Christians to spot, you begin to recognize just how well it works.

And if you know of people in need, it's only natural to want to expose them to that kind of power. Praying for other people is one of the most important ministries available to you. What better way is there to show your love for others than bringing their needs before the Lord?

Word

Praying for other people is called *intercession*. You'll probably never have a reason to use that word in a sentence, but it's always good to know for trivia.

You don't have to look very far in the Bible to see intercession in action. Genesis 18 tells the story of Abraham, who went to God to talk about his nephew Lot. Lot and his family were living in the city of Sodom. Unfortunately, Sodom was ground zero for God's judgment against wickedness. The Lord was getting ready to rain fire down on the city to destroy it and its citizens.

Read about the way Abraham approached God with his concern for Lot:

> Then the men rose from there and looked toward Sodom, and Abraham went with them to send them on the way. And the LORD said, "Shall I hide from Abraham what I am doing, since Abraham shall surely become a great and mighty nation, and all the nations of the earth shall be blessed in him? For I have known him, in order that he may command his children and his household after him, that they keep the way of the LORD, to do righteousness and justice, that the LORD may bring to Abraham what He has spoken to him." And the LORD said, "Because the outcry against Sodom and Gomorrah is great, and because their sin is very

grave, I will go down now and see whether they have done altogether according to the outcry against it that has come to Me; and if not, I will know."

Then the men turned away from there and went toward Sodom, but Abraham still stood before the Lord. And Abraham came near and said, "Would You also destroy the righteous with the wicked? Suppose there were fifty righteous within the city; would You also destroy the place and not spare it for the fifty righteous that were in it? Far be it from You to do such a thing as this, to slay the righteous with the wicked, so that the righteous should be as the wicked; far be it from You! Shall not the Judge of all the earth do right?" So the Lord said, "If I find in Sodom fifty righteous within the city, then I will spare all the place for their sakes." Then Abraham answered and said, "Indeed now, I who am but dust and ashes have taken it upon myself to speak to the Lord: Suppose there were five less than the fifty righteous; would You destroy all of the city for lack of five?" So He said, "If I find there forty-five, I will not destroy it." And he spoke to Him yet again and said, "Suppose there should be forty found there?" So He said, "I will not do it for the sake of forty." Then he said, "Let not the Lord be angry, and I will speak: Suppose thirty should be found there?" So He said, "I will not do it if I find thirty there." And he said, "Indeed now, I have taken it upon myself to speak to the Lord: Suppose twenty should be found there?" So He said, "I will not destroy it for the sake of twenty." Then he said, "Let not the

Lord be angry, and I will speak but once more:
Suppose ten should be found there?" And He said, "I
will not destroy it for the sake of ten." So the LORD
went His way as soon as He had finished speaking
with Abraham; and Abraham returned to his place.
(Gen. 18:16–33)

Man, talk about putting yourself on the line! Abraham
knew that the lower the number went, the better chance his
nephew Lot had of escaping the firestorm. But he also knew
he was walking a tightrope. The more he nagged, the more
he ran the risk of making God angry. Abraham must have
been scared out of his sandals, but he kept going back to
God again and again for Lot's sake.

Abraham wasn't trying to push God as far as he could.
The last thing he wanted to do was to tick God off. But he
was the type of guy who would give everything to help
others. The kind of dedication and concern that Abraham
showed is the kind we need in our prayers.

And don't miss the way God responded to Abraham. He
knew Abe was praying out of concern for a loved one, so He
showed all the patience in the world. By agreeing to lower more
and more the minimum requirements, He was showing
Abraham that He, too, was concerned about Lot and his family.

And what about the psalmists? you may be wondering.
*Those guys had prayers for every occasion. Surely they did their
share of "intercessing" (or whatever you call it).*

As a matter of fact, they did. When the psalmists prayed,
a major concern was their nation. They knew that Israel
didn't exactly have a great reputation in God's eyes, so they

spent a pretty good chunk of their prayer time asking Him
to forgive, rescue, restore, and bless their nation.

Here's a good example of the way they prayed:

LORD, You have been favorable to Your land;
You have brought back the captivity of Jacob.
You have forgiven the iniquity of Your people;
You have covered all their sin. Selah
You have taken away all Your wrath;
You have turned from the fierceness of Your anger.
Restore us, O God of our salvation,
And cause Your anger toward us to cease.
Will You be angry with us forever?
Will You prolong Your anger to all generations?
Will You not revive us again,
That Your people may rejoice in You?
Show us Your mercy, LORD,
And grant us Your salvation. (Ps. 85:1–7)

Notice that the psalmist kicked off his prayer by mentioning what the Lord had *already* done for the nation. He gave the
Lord respect and credit before bringing more requests to Him.
That's a pattern you'll want to keep in mind when you pray for
other people. Always try to start with praise for what God has
already done in those people's lives.

The apostle Paul was also big on intercession. Most of his
books in the New Testament contain prayers or references to
prayers for other people:

First, I thank my God through Jesus Christ for you
all, that your faith is spoken of throughout the whole

world. For God is my witness, whom I serve with my spirit in the gospel of His Son, that without ceasing I make mention of you always in my prayers, making request if, by some means, now at last I may find a way in the will of God to come to you. (Rom. 1:8–10)

The Roman, Corinthian, Ephesian, Philippian, and Colossian Christians were all on Paul's prayer list. Paul knew that prayer was his most important tool to help his fellow believers, so he used it every chance he had.

Christians throughout history have continued to make intercession part of their everyday Christian walk. Check out these classic prayers:

We bring before you, O Lord, the troubles and perils of people and nations, the sighing of prisoners and captives, the sorrows of the bereaved, the necessities of strangers, the helplessness of the weak, the despondency of the weary, the failing powers of the aged. O Lord, draw near to each; for the sake of Jesus Christ, our Lord. (Saint Anselm, 1033–1109)

Dear Lord, for all in pain
We pray to thee;
O come and smite again
Thine enemy.

Give to thy servants skill
To soothe and bless,
And to the tired and ill

Give quietness.
And, Lord, to those who know
Pain may not cease,
Come near, that even so
They may have peace. (Amy Carmichael, 1868–1951)

These are just a few of the models we have when it comes to praying for others. You might call them some of intercession's greatest hits. If some of these prayers really hit home for you, try praying them. Or you might borrow the parts that are especially meaningful to you and rework them to create your own version. At the very least, these prayers and passages should give you an idea of just how important it is for you to pray for others.

→ HEADS UP

Here's a not-so-obvious prayer tip straight from Jesus Himself: "I say to you that if two of you agree on earth concerning anything that they ask, it will be done for them by My Father in heaven. For where two or three are gathered together in My name, I am there in the midst of them" (Matt. 18:19–20).

The idea in these verses is not that God ignores someone alone who comes to Him. These verses suggest that there's something special about two or more people getting together for a common cause.

If you have a prayer request that's really important to you, try calling in some backup. Find two or three Christian friends, explain your request, and ask them to pray about it with you.

You may choose to pray all together or alone, or you may pray in shifts so that one person is always praying throughout a certain period of time.

What's it to You?

If you care enough about your friends, family, and even people you don't know to ask God to get involved in their lives, then you owe it to them and yourself to do it right. Here are some tips to keep in mind when you take prayer requests for others to the Lord.

get your facts straight

The more you know about a person, the better you can pray for him. That doesn't mean you need to run a background check on everyone you mention to God. But it does mean you should take your requests—the people you pray for—seriously.

Think of praying as you would giving a presentation in front of a group. You can come in cold, wing it, and hope for the best, or you can come in prepared, lay out what you know, and nail it. It's up to you . . . and God. And as far as we know, God's never gotten upset with anyone for preparing too much for prayer.

Here's what it comes down to. If you take prayer seriously (and obviously you do, or you wouldn't be reading this book) and you care enough about someone to get God involved in her life, then it's only natural that you'd want to find out as much as possible for your prayers.

The best way to find out what's going on in someone's life

is to talk to the person. Duh, right? Not necessarily. That doesn't mean you should just walk up to your friends and ask, "Hey, what do you want me to pray about for you?" Depending on who you're tight with, some of your friends might answer you truthfully, and others might freak.

Remember, not everyone thinks God and prayer are as cool as you think they are. Some people might think that you're trying to change them with your prayers, that you don't like them the way they are. Others might accuse you of thinking that you're better or more spiritual than they are or of praying just to make yourself look good. Still others might treat you as if you're a religious fanatic trying to shove God down their throats.

So unless you know for sure that someone would appreciate your prayers, it's probably best not to mention that you're praying for him—at least not right away. Instead, keep your ears open whenever you're around him. Learn to listen "between the lines" when he talks to find out how he's feeling and what he's facing in life.

You might even want to keep a prayer notebook handy so that when you get a minute or two to yourself, you can jot down any needs or requests you stumble across.

Don't misunderstand, though. There's no rule that says you need to have X amount of information about a person before you can pray for him. It's a good idea, but it's not like the eleventh commandment or anything.

Even if you haven't got a clue about what's going on in someone's life, you can still pray for that person. There are times when it's okay to say, "Lord, I'm not sure what's going on with Clem today, but please help him."

You can even get more specific if you want. You can say, "Lord, please guide Clem in the decisions he has to make today," or "God, please give Clem a sense of peace in any area that might be worrying him." Praying for guidance and a sense of peace is like giving cash for Christmas. It's always appreciated, and everyone can use it.

give god room to work

Praying for God to work in someone's life is cool. Telling God what to do in that person's life isn't. If that seems pretty obvious to you, you may be surprised at how easy it is to cross the line between cool and not so cool. When you pray for someone—especially for someone you really care about and know well—you may be tempted to believe you know what's best for the person.

The problem is, you don't know what the person really needs. And neither does the person you're praying for. Since only God knows what's going on inside and outside, only *He* can decide what is best for that person.

The way you look at people's situations and the way God looks at them are completely different. For example, based on what you know, you might be okay with sending up prayer requests like these:

- "Please help Dad to get the promotion to vice president that he deserves."
- "Please don't let Jamal's grandmother die of cancer. You know how close Jamal is to her. If she dies, he'll never get over it."
- "Please let Ryan get in to Yale."

- "Help Kala see that the guy she's dating is a player and that she needs to get rid of him."

You may not know that

- the stress of being a vice president would make your dad's life miserable and cause him serious heart problems.
- Jamal is already suffering every day because he sees his grandmother in such pain all the time. His grandmother has told him she's ready to die, and Jamal is learning to accept it.
- the University of Minnesota has a program better suited for Ryan's ultimate career choice, even though Ryan doesn't even know what that choice is yet.
- the guy Kala is dating is just immature. He has the potential to become an ideal husband and father.

Kind of helps to have the big picture, doesn't it? Until you do, you're just guessing at what's best for the people you pray for. Instead of trying to come up with your own solutions, you're always better off asking God to show you His. God isn't going to hit the "mute" button on your prayers for other people if you get a little carried away and offer suggestions of your own. But He refuses to be restricted by your ideas of what's good for people.

> only when we ask God to work can we delight in seeing him answer our prayers.

It's a fine line, you see, between the one extreme of trying to dictate to God exactly what we want and the other extreme of not being specific enough in our requests. We can't just throw out a huge, blanket prayer like this: "God, please take care of all the unsaved people in the world and anyone who's hungry." It's always good to be specific in what you ask for. Pray for people by name, by need, and with a purpose. Only when we ask God to work can we delight in seeing Him answer our prayers. That's how we join Him in what He's doing.

If you want to pray effectively for other people, try not to focus on "fixing" their circumstances. Instead, concentrate on their heart attitudes. For example, instead of asking God to help Trish find a boyfriend so that she won't be lonely anymore, try asking Him to help her deal with her insecurities that cause the loneliness.

get your hands dirty

Prayer—especially passionate prayer—is not a white-collar job. Look at the words on the cover of this book again: *Igniting Your Life with Passionate Prayer*. Passionate prayer is blue-collar work. There's nothing fancy about it. There's nothing passionate about sitting in your house and saying a few words to God on other people's behalf. Halfhearted, wimpy, faithless prayers won't do any igniting in this lifetime.

To maximize your prayer life, you've got to be ready to get your hands dirty. If you're not willing to get involved in the lives of the people you pray for, all you're really doing is dumping work on God's desk. It's as if you're saying, "Here, God, take care of this for me."

A better way to approach your role is to ask, "Lord, how do

You want to use me in this situation?" or, "What can I do to be part of Your will in this person's life?" It's the difference between trying to direct God and letting Him direct you.

For example . . .

Brian, a computer programmer, was recently assigned to a new project. His partner on the project is a designer named Ken. Based on the way Ken talked about God during one of their discussions, it's pretty obvious to Brian that he's not a Christian. Brian, who is a Christian, has never said anything to Ken about it because he doesn't want to screw up their working relationship. But Brian is concerned about Ken's spiritual life.

> extreme pray-ers offer more than their words to God; they offer themselves.

Brian can pray, "Please help Ken to understand why he needs to accept Christ as his Savior," or he can pray, "Please give me the right words to say to Ken to get him thinking about spiritual things, the patience to handle his sarcastic responses, and the wisdom to answer his questions as well as I can."

Here's another one:

Heather recently watched a documentary on the horrible conditions in eastern Africa. Scene after scene of starving children and dead bodies left her shaken up physically, emotionally, and spiritually. Days later, she still can't get the images out of her mind.

Heather can pray, "Please help the starving children in Africa," or she can pray, "Please help me find an organization that I can give my money and time to so that I can make a difference in the lives of these kids."

Both prayers are valuable. We should pray for God's intervention because some things only God can do. But whenever we have a chance to pray *and* do something specific to help, we should. Extreme pray-ers offer more than their words to God; they offer themselves. In their prayers, they identify people's needs. In their actions, they leave themselves open to be used by God, however He sees fit.

When it comes to passionate prayer, your job isn't over when you say "Amen." Instead, it's just beginning.

one last thing

I kicked off this chapter with some real-life answers to prayer. If you think it's cool to read about people's lives being changed by prayer, just wait until you experience it first-hand. One of the perks of being an extreme pray-er is that you often have a front-row seat for God's response.

Praying for other people makes you part of their lives. When God answers those prayers, you get to experience the thrill along with the people you prayed for.

taking it to heart

Time to put the ol' gray matter to work. Knowing how to pray wisely for other people isn't a skill you're born with. Discovering the meaning of true intercession takes time and a willingness to learn from your mistakes. To help you in your quest, consider the following questions. If you want to really master intercession, you'll need to put some serious thought into your answers.

1. Have you ever seen an unmistakable answer to prayer in the life of someone you know? If so, what happened? What was your first reaction when you heard about it? How did it affect your attitude toward prayer?

2. What is your longest-running prayer request that involves someone other than yourself? How long have you been praying for that person? How long will you continue to pray?

3. What questions could you ask to find out how to pray for someone without putting her on the spot or making her uncomfortable?

4. Give an example of praying cluelessly for someone else. (Bonus points if the example comes from your own life.)

5. How can you "get your hands dirty" when it comes to the people you're praying for right now?

6. Write down the names of three people you know who need prayer this week. Next to each name, write a specific prayer request for that person.

7. What changes are you going to make to your prayer habits to improve the way you pray for other people? Be as specific as possible in your answer.

One from the heart

Based on what you've learned about intercession and what you've read of the prayers other people have offered, write your own prayer to God. Be sure to share your thoughts and feelings about what's going on in the lives of other people. And try to be as specific as possible throughout your prayer.

7

WHEN I FIND MYSELF IN TIMES OF TROUBLE

Don't travel late at night. That's what everyone told me, Lisa reminded herself. *But did I listen? Nooooo. The clock on the dashboard flashed 2:15 A.M. The eerie quiet of the deserted stretch of Indiana highway was interrupted only by the rhythmic clicking of the emergency blinkers and the hiss of the steam that poured out from underneath the hood. Lisa thought desperately through her situation: no phone, no gas stations or restaurants for at least ten miles, nothing to protect herself with except a rolled-up road map, and no clue about what to do next. Just then a pair of headlights lit up the road behind her. Lisa's heart jumped, partly out of hope but mostly out of fear. As the car got closer, Lisa could see it slow down. Her heart started pounding. The car, which turned out to be a pickup truck, pulled up right behind her. Lisa was shaking. "Please, God," she prayed . . .*

❋   ❋   ❋

"Good morning," the doctor said as he took a seat right next to the examining table where Steve was sitting. Steve tried to respond but found that his throat was too dry. So he just nodded. "I'm afraid I have bad news for you, Steve," the doctor said. "The tests came back positive. It's prostate cancer, and we're concerned that it may have spread." He said something else about aggressive treatment and worst-case scenarios, but Steve could barely concentrate. He was thinking of his wife and his nine-month-old twins at home. His wife hadn't slept for three days, worrying about his appointment. Steve had promised her that he was okay, and he couldn't imagine how he was going to tell her he wasn't. Right in front of the doctor, Steve bowed his head and closed his eyes. "Oh, Lord," he began . . .

it's like this

For most people, praying during emergencies or times of serious trouble is more of an instinct than something they learn. Think about it. How do you give someone tips on communicating to God during desperate times?

Step 1: Drop to your knees.

Step 2: Shout, "Help me, God!"

Step 3: Repeat Steps 1 and 2 if necessary.

Not much skill or knowledge needed, right?

The one thing you need to remember is that when you're in trouble, regardless of the problem, any prayer you can squeeze out is better than none at all. It's important to maintain contact with God, no matter how shaky that connection may seem at times. If you stick with God, He will see you through whatever you're facing.

Word

All kinds of troubles call for all kinds of prayers. You could spend a month trying to identify them all. Instead, let's focus on the types of troubles that you're most likely to face: doubt, fear, and pain.

doubt

Hebrews 11:1 tells us that "faith is the substance of things hoped for, the evidence of things not seen." Sometimes, though, not being able to see what's going on in your life can mess with your mind. Depending on what's going on in your life, you may even start to doubt some things that you thought were rock-solid beliefs. Maybe you doubt whether God will provide for your needs. Maybe you doubt whether God really loves you. Maybe you doubt whether God is really good.

If doubts are starting to creep into your thinking, remember two things. First, don't freak. Having doubts doesn't make you a bad person; it makes you a thinking person. More often than not, having doubts ends up strengthening beliefs rather than tearing them down.

The second thing to remember when you're struggling with doubt is to keep praying. That may seem to be a weird thing to do, since prayer is probably one of the things that you have doubts about. But it's important to pray through your doubts. Even if you don't have complete confidence in God as you pray, that's okay. He doesn't need your complete confidence to accomplish His will.

In time, you'll start to notice traces of God's work in your life, answered prayers here and there, that will make it easier for you to shake your doubts.

When you take your doubts to God, be honest—brutally honest if you need to—about what you're feeling. God's okay with that. He can handle your truthful feelings without getting angry or feeling rejected. Your doubts aren't going to affect His self-image, so speak your mind.

Some of the most devoted Christians of all time struggled with doubt at some point or another. Check out these prayers from centuries past:

> Lord, make possible for me by grace what is impossible to me by nature. You know that I am not able to endure very much, and that I am downcast by the slightest difficulty. Grant that for your sake I may come to love and desire any hardship that puts me to the test, for salvation is brought to my soul when I undergo suffering and trouble for you. (Thomas à Kempis, 1379–1471)

> O Holy Spirit, give me faith that will protect me from despair, from passions and from vice, give me such love for God as will blot out all hatred and bitterness, give me the hope that will deliver me from fear and faint heartedness. (Dietrich Bonhoeffer, 1906–45)

Although these major-league Christians had doubts, they knew that prayer was the answer. Even at their lowest points, they had confidence that the Lord could do something about their lack of belief.

Do you need a solution to get rid of your doubt? The best advice comes from Psalm 46:

Be still, and know that I am God;
I will be exalted among the nations,
I will be exalted in the earth! (v. 10)

Patience—that's the key. No matter what happens that makes you doubt, it can't change the fact that God is all-powerful. If you wait patiently long enough, you will see evidence of His power in your life.

The apostle Paul gave us one more assurance that we can cling to when doubt strikes: "For I am persuaded that neither death nor life, nor angels nor principalities nor powers, nor things present nor things to come, nor height nor depth, nor any other created thing, shall be able to separate us from the love of God which is in Christ Jesus our Lord" (Rom. 8:38–39).

> whether you feel close to him or not, you can be sure that he's always close to you.

Read that list again. It doesn't leave much room for anything to drive a wedge between you and God. So whether you feel close to Him or not, you can be sure that He's always close to you. The way to discover His closeness is prayer—extreme prayer.

fear

Fear isn't just for wusses. No matter how tough you think you are, somewhere, sometime you're going to face a situation that really throws you. You'll feel overwhelmed by a situation that you simply can't control. The question you have to ask in advance is, What am I going to do when it happens?

Your answer will depend on your situation. If you're in immediate danger—if you're scared for your physical safety because of where you are or who you're with—send up a 911 prayer. ("God, please help me now!") Desperate situations call for desperate measures. You might also ask God to give you a clear head and a heart of courage to help you do whatever needs to be done.

Usually, though, the biggest fears you'll face don't involve immediate danger. Instead, they're the fears that grow over time. Alison, for example, remembers being afraid that her parents would get a divorce. The older she got and the more she saw her mom and dad fight, the more frightened she became. By the time she was a sophomore in high school, her fears were affecting her health. She developed eating and sleeping problems. Some of her friends stopped hanging out with her because they said she had flipped out.

Alison tried praying about her situation. Sometimes she prayed for God to fix her family, with a mom and dad who loved each other and who gave her all the love, support, and encouragement she needed. Sometimes she prayed for her parents to remember why they fell in love in the first place. Sometimes she prayed that they would just stop fighting until after she moved out and went to college.

After about two years of praying, Alison finally realized that her fears were controlling her life. She decided to stop praying for her parents' marriage to be saved and to start praying about the way it was affecting her. She asked God to help her get rid of the "spirit of fear" she read about in 2 Timothy 1:7. Gradually her attitude changed. The thought of her parents' divorce still scared her, but it wasn't ruining her life as it had before.

A couple of years later, when her parents did divorce, Alison was sad but not devastated. She wasn't nearly as frightened as she thought she'd be. She was surprised that yes, she could get through this.

That's just one example of prayer in action in the midst of scary times.

Maybe you're facing a fear that you need to pray about. Open your Bible first to see if you can find a few examples or words of wisdom to follow. The good news is, you won't have to look far to find them. Almost all of the major characters in the Bible had to deal with fear at one time or another.

Moses is a good example. He was out watching over a flock of sheep one day when God appeared to him in the form of a burning bush and dropped a bombshell:

> And the LORD said: "I have surely seen the oppression of My people who are in Egypt, and have heard their cry because of their taskmasters, for I know their sorrows. So I have come down to deliver them out of the hand of the Egyptians, and to bring them up from that land to a good and large land, to a land flowing with milk and honey, to the place of the Canaanites and the Hittites and the Amorites and the Perizzites and the Hivites and the Jebusites. Now therefore, behold, the cry of the children of Israel has come to Me, and I have also seen the oppression with which the

Egyptians oppress them. Come now, therefore, and I will send you to Pharaoh that you may bring My people, the children of Israel, out of Egypt." But Moses said to God, "Who am I that I should go to Pharaoh, and that I should bring the children of Israel out of Egypt?" So He said, "I will certainly be with you. And this shall be a sign to you that I have sent you: When you have brought the people out of Egypt, you shall serve God on this mountain." Then Moses said to God, "Indeed, when I come to the children of Israel and say to them, 'The God of your fathers has sent me to you,' and they say to me, 'What is His name?' what shall I say to them?" And God said to Moses, "I AM WHO I AM." And He said, "Thus you shall say to the children of Israel, 'I AM has sent me to you.'" . . .

Then Moses answered and said, "But suppose they will not believe me or listen to my voice; suppose they say, 'The LORD has not appeared to you.'" So the LORD said to him, "What is that in your hand?" He said, "A rod." And He said, "Cast it on the ground." So he cast it on the ground, and it became a serpent; and Moses fled from it. Then the LORD said to Moses, "Reach out your hand and take it by the tail" (and he reached out his hand and caught it, and it became a rod in his hand), "that they may believe that the LORD God of their fathers, the God of Abraham, the God of Isaac, and the God of Jacob, has appeared to you." . . .

Then Moses said to the LORD, "O my Lord, I am not eloquent, neither before nor since You have spoken to Your servant; but I am slow of speech and slow of tongue." So the LORD said to him, "Who has made man's mouth? Or who makes the mute, the deaf, the seeing, or the blind? Have not I, the LORD? Now therefore, go, and I will be with your mouth and teach you what you shall say." But he said, "O my Lord, please send by the hand of whomever else You may send." (Ex. 3:7–14; 4:1–5, 10–13)

Can you imagine being in Moses' sandals? You're minding your own business with a bunch of sheep one day when God appears out of nowhere and says, "Hey, you! Yeah, I mean *you*, Moses! You know those millions of Israelites who are being held as slaves in Egypt? You're going in to rescue them."

Is it any wonder Moses froze up?

In his conversation with God, Moses wasn't shy about letting God know how afraid he was. He tried different excuses with God, hoping to get Him to change His mind:

- "Pharaoh won't listen to me."
- "The people of Israel won't believe You sent me."
- "I'm not a good public speaker."
- "I'm not ready to go."

Of course, Moses was really saying, "Please, God, don't make me do it!"

And get a load of how God responded to him. He didn't drag Moses over to the bush and start smacking sense into him. He didn't call him a wimp and start making fun of him. He didn't even bawl him out for arguing.

No, each time Moses gave God a frightened excuse about

why he couldn't lead the Israelites, God listened patiently, reassured him, and promised to be with him.

It's the same way He responds to our fears.

What that means for you is that you can use Moses' conversation as a model for sharing your deepest fears and insecurities with God. Don't worry about what God will think of you or how He'll respond. Just get everything out so that you can deal with it together.

To do that, you'll have to figure out what's really scaring you. For example, if you asked me what my greatest fear is, I'd probably tell you it's speaking in front of a crowd. But if I thought about it for a while, I'd probably realize that that's only part of it. My real fear is more about embarrassing myself in public.

So I could ask God to protect me from all situations in which I might be forced to speak in front of a crowd, but I wouldn't be addressing my fear. I'd be addressing only a part of it. If I asked God to help me overcome my fear of embarrassing myself, He might very well put me in front of crowds for the rest of my life to do just that.

When you pray about your fears, you can expect God to do something about them, though it might not be quite what you want Him to do. God's not going to leave you at the mercy of your fears. He's going to help you face them down and (eventually) overcome them. If you doubt that, check out the rest of the book of Exodus. Guess who you'll find leading the Israelites out of Egypt and toward the promised land? That's right, Moses—the ex-coward.

What about the psalmists? you may be wondering. *They've shown up in every other chapter of this book. Didn't they have their share of fears too?*

You bet they did. And they dealt with them in the same way they dealt with all of their emotions. They prayed about them. Here is a prayer David wrote when he was struggling with fear:

> My heart is severely pained within me,
> And the terrors of death have fallen upon me.
> Fearfulness and trembling have come upon me,
> And horror has overwhelmed me.
> So I said, "Oh, that I had wings like a dove!
> I would fly away and be at rest.
> Indeed, I would wander far off,
> And remain in the wilderness. Selah
> I would hasten my escape
> From the windy storm and tempest." (Ps. 55:4–8)

Terrors of death. Fearfulness and trembling. Horror. You'd expect to find those words in a preview for a horror film, not in a prayer.

David was letting it all out in this psalm. He was saying, "God, if I had my choice right now, I'd be out of here as fast as my feet can carry me. I'm scared to death, and I need to escape."

Does that reaction seem familiar to you? How many times have you thought about running away from your problems and escaping for a while?

A time comes, though, when you have to make the decision to turn your fears over to God and trust Him to do what's ultimately best for you. If you talk to people who've confronted their fears of . . .

revealing their inner selves to others,

being alone,

taking risks,

experiencing failure,

confronting people who are intimidating,

. . . then they'll probably tell you that it was the hardest thing they ever had to do. And then they'll tell you how glad they are they did it and how much more fulfilling their lives are because they're not disabled by fear anymore.

Honestly facing your fears in prayer is one of the hardest things you'll ever do. But the more committed you are to facing them, the more extreme your prayer life will become. When your prayer life shifts into extreme mode, you're in for the ride of your life.

pain

The ugly truth is that nobody gets out of this world unscathed. Sooner or later, we're all going to experience pain, whether it's physical, emotional, or both. When you come face-to-face with suffering, you have two prayer options available to you.

First, you can ask the Lord to take away the pain. There's nothing wrong with praying that way as long as you're prepared to deal with the fact that God may not honor your request—at least, not right away. Like it or not, pain and suffering can produce incredible spiritual and emotional growth. The feelings that you face when you're hurting can stretch you in ways you can't imagine. Having firsthand experience with pain also allows you to empathize with others who are hurting, giving you the opportunity to help them in meaningful ways.

Second, you can ask the Lord to give you wisdom, strength, and a sense of His presence in the midst of your pain. If you recognize that some pain and suffering are inevitable in your life, you can prepare yourself for the reality. Ask God to give you the wisdom to understand what good will eventually come from the suffering, the strength to keep going when things get really bad, and the sense of His presence to keep you from feeling alone in your pain.

The author of Psalm 66 obviously had personal experience with pain and suffering. But he was determined not to let his pain have the last word. He knew that there was something beyond his suffering. He wrote to the Lord:

> For You, O God, have tested us;
> You have refined us as silver is refined.
> You brought us into the net;
> You laid affliction on our backs.
> You have caused men to ride over our heads;
> We went through fire and through water;
> But You brought us out to rich fulfillment. (vv. 10–12)

The psalmist knew that no matter how bad his suffering became, the Lord could turn it into something good. He might not have known exactly what the Lord was going to do, but he trusted Him. He gave God the benefit of the doubt in his prayer. When you take your suffering to the Lord, make sure that you give Him the same consideration.

One of the most amazing prayers of pain ever recorded came from Jesus Himself the night He was arrested. Jesus knew that in a matter of hours He would be nailed to a cross and cut off from everyone He loved as He paid the price for the sins of the entire world.

Before that happened, though, Jesus talked with His heavenly Father. Here's how Matthew described the scene:

> Then Jesus came with them to a place called Gethsemane, and said to the disciples, "Sit here while I go and pray over there." And He took with Him Peter and the two sons of Zebedee, and He began to be sorrowful and deeply distressed. Then He said to them, "My soul is exceedingly sorrowful, even to death. Stay here and watch with Me." He went a little farther and fell on His face, and prayed, saying, "O My Father, if it is possible, let this cup pass from Me; nevertheless, not as I will, but as You will." (Matt. 26:36–39)

How incredible is this prayer?

Look at the way Jesus poured out His feelings to God. He laid His emotions and pain bare before His Father. He said, "If there's a way to do this other than the Cross, please let Me know now."

But Jesus didn't stop there. He closed His prayer by turning everything over to God's will. He said, "I've told You what I would like to happen, Father. Now tell Me what You want to happen."

That's the way all passionate prayers, whether they come from doubt, fear, pain, or even happiness, should end—"Not my will, but Yours be done, God."

What's it to you?

Since no two people's problems are identical, there's no

formula for a general solution to overcome your problems. But you can definitely try some proven techniques.

get involved in your recovery

When you're in trouble, the best thing you can do is pray. But that's not the only thing you should do. Getting God involved in your troubles doesn't give you the right to kick back and wait for Him to make everything better. You have to be willing to face your situation head-on and do your part. God will bless your sincere efforts to overcome your doubt, fear, and pain. But He won't allow you to pull your head inside your shell like a turtle and just hope for the best.

If you're struggling with doubt, you've got to do some work to figure out how to overcome it. Make an appointment to talk to your pastor or a trusted Christian leader. Find relevant books at your church library or a Christian bookstore. Immerse yourself in Bible stories in which people had to deal with their doubts.

HEADS UP

The most famous doubter in the Bible is Thomas, the disciple who wouldn't believe that Jesus had risen from the dead until he had physical proof. John 20:24–29 tells us that Thomas was absent the first time Jesus appeared to His disciples after His death.

When the other disciples tried to tell Tom what happened, he said, "Unless I see in His hands the print of the nails, and put my hand into His side, I will not believe."

We could rag on old doubting Thomas all day for his lack of faith, but that's not really the point of this story. The point is that Jesus was willing to meet Thomas's demands in order to help him overcome his doubt. The next time Jesus appeared to the disciples, He basically told Thomas, "Hey, if touching My scars is what you need, go ahead and touch."

What better proof is there that the Lord isn't threatened by doubt? The fact is, He's willing to go to extremes to help us work through our doubts if we truly desire to overcome them.

If you're struggling with fears, you've got to take the necessary steps to either overcome them or learn to live with them. Spend some time thinking about why you're afraid and how your fear is affecting your life. Try taking baby steps toward confronting your fear. (For example, you may be scared of speaking in front of large crowds, so try leading a small prayer group or Bible study group. When you become comfortable with that, move on to a larger Sunday school class, and so on.) If the fears you're dealing with are especially disabling, make an appointment to talk to a professional counselor.

If you're dealing with pain, talk to someone about it. Depending on what kind of pain you're experiencing and how it's affecting you, go to a trusted friend or a professional counselor, and share your feelings. Don't try to shut out others from your situation. And don't let your pride stop you from admitting that you need help.

use what you learn to help others

No matter what problems you're facing, you're not alone. In fact, you'd probably be surprised at the number of people you know who are struggling with similar problems. Those people really need someone to tell them—from personal experience—how to work through their situations and what mistakes to avoid along the way.

So if you've experienced God's work in your life—if He's helped you deal with doubts, conquer fears, or overcome pain—you've got a responsibility to share your experience with others. Maybe you're not a "people person." Maybe the idea of being a mentor to someone else seems ridiculous to you. Get over it. The thing is, you have no idea what you have to offer someone until you actually start talking to the person.

So how do you hook up with others who might need your help? First, ask God to do the matchmaking. Pray for Him to bring people into your life who could benefit from what you've gone through. Then ask Him to give you the wisdom and sensitivity to know what to say and how to say it.

Second, open up about your struggles and experiences with as many people as possible. Eric and Kara suffered three miscarriages in their quest to have a baby. Before the miscarriages, Eric had been a keep-to-himself kind of guy. He rarely went out of his way to talk to people and never talked about his feelings.

Since the miscarriages, though, Eric has felt the need to open up and share his experiences with as many people as possible. What's happened since then is that men he barely knows invite him to lunch or call him at home just to talk about their experiences with miscarriage. Even though Eric had never thought of himself as a ministering type of guy, ever since his decision to go public with his pain, that's just what he's become.

Who's to say God doesn't want to do the same thing with you?

one last thing

If there's one thing you should take away from this chapter, it's this: never underestimate God's ability to see you through any situation. No matter how extreme your doubt, fear, or pain seems, it's no match for God's healing power.

> never underestimate God's ability to see you through any situation.

Passionate prayer is the kind that continues, even when you don't necessarily feel like praying. Passionate prayer is the kind you offer up because you don't know what else to do. Passionate prayer is what brings God into your darkest moments. Passionate prayer is what will ultimately change your life.

taking it to heart

Time to put the ol' gray matter to work. Figuring out how to involve God in your daily problems and struggles takes practice. To give you a better idea, think through the following questions. If an extreme prayer life is your goal, you'll need to put some time and thought into your answers.

1. What are some common mistakes that people make when it comes to praying in times of trouble?

2. Of all the Bible stories you know about God's helping someone in trouble, which ones mean the most to you personally? Why are those stories so important to you?

3. Write down three questions about doubt, fear, and pain that you would like to have answered.

4. Write down the names of three mature Christians whom you can ask for answers to those questions.

5. What are some doubts you've faced? How have you overcome them?

6. What are some fears you've faced? How have you overcome them?

7. What are the most painful situations you've faced? How did you get through them?

8. Write down three things you can do this week to deal with the problems you're facing.

One from the heart

Based on what you've learned about doubt, fear, and pain and what you've read of the prayers in this chapter, write your own prayer to God. Be sure to share your thoughts and feelings about a problem you're facing right now. And try to be as specific as possible throughout your prayer.

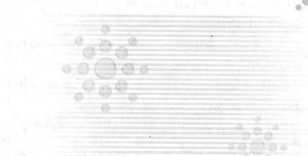

8

ONE TO GROW ON

"You've really changed, you know that?"

Sam stopped and looked back. Josh Evans was walking across the parking lot toward him.

"You talking to me?" Sam asked.

"Yeah," Josh said. "We were all talking about you. We were saying how much you've changed since we started the prayer group. It's like you're a totally different person from what you were eight months ago."

"Hey, maybe I put on some weight, but don't insult me," Sam joked.

"No, seriously," Josh said. "Do you remember the first time we all met to pray?"

"Is that the time I prayed for more hot-looking chicks to come to church?" Sam asked.

"Yeah, that's the one."

"I'm surprised you guys didn't kick me out after that one,"

Sam said, smiling at the memory. "So why do you think I've changed?"

"I don't know," Josh said. "The way you pray is different. The things you talk about are different. I tried to tell everyone else that it was my good influence rubbing off on you, but they all shot me down."

"Yeah, I look at prayer differently now," Sam explained. "I mean, when you guys first asked me to join a prayer group, I figured it was an easy way to get in good with God. I didn't want to be spiritual or anything. I just wanted to work the system. You know, 'Ask, and you will receive.' Well, I wanted to talk Him into a new sports car."

"Hey, you came close," Josh said, pointing to Sam's beat-up Ford.

"Yeah, well," Sam said with a laugh. "When I first found out that prayer wasn't what I thought it was going to be, I was like, 'Gee, what a waste of time.' But then I kept going with it and found out that it's a hundred times more incredible than I ever imagined."

"I can't believe this is you talking," Josh said.

"Tell me about it," Sam replied. "When we first started the group, I used to blow off my prayer time every day. Now if I forget to pray during the day, it's like I forgot to eat. I can feel that something's missing."

"I think that's called spiritual maturity."

"Whatever," Sam said. "What's really weird, though, is that people are starting to ask me to pray in front of groups."

"That's what happens when you take God seriously," Josh said. "People recognize it and want to plug into it. You've got to admit, it's pretty cool to have people respect the way you live."

"Yeah, I guess it is," Sam said.

it's like this

Have you ever noticed the way married couples and even good friends become more and more alike the longer they're together? It's a natural process. If you spend enough time with someone, that person's mannerisms, habits, sense of humor, and ways of thinking are bound to rub off on you eventually.

The same thing happens in prayer. If you spend enough time in conversation with God, eventually His way of thinking, His priorities, and His love are going to have an effect on you and the way you live. The more extreme your prayer life is, the more extreme the effect will be.

If you want to put a name on it, you could call these changes spiritual growth. It doesn't happen overnight. In fact, you may not even notice it for weeks, months, or even years after you start your quest for an intense prayer life. There's a good chance that other people will pick up on it before you do. You may notice subtle changes in the way people—especially other Christians—look at you.

You'll probably find yourself being offered more opportunities to be involved in different ministries. Depending on the circumstances, some people may even look to you to assume a leadership role. At that point, things tend to snowball. The more people recognize your spiritual development, the more they will seek you out when needs arise.

Look, your pastor isn't going to turn over Sunday morning services to you or anything like that. But as your spiritual life changes as a result of spending consistent quality time with God in prayer, your role in the family of God will change as well.

That's what passionate prayer can do. The only thing that competes with prayer for the effect it has on your spiritual life is spending time in God's Word.

So that raises an obvious question: What would happen if you incorporated Bible study into your prayer life? The answer? Prepare to have your spiritual life rocked.

Word

We can find everything God want us to know about Him and our relationship with Him in His Word. The Bible reveals God's heart, what He wants for us—and from us. When you use the Bible as part of your prayer life, you form an immediate bond with God. Using Scripture in your prayers gives you a clearer understanding of where God is coming from. What's more, you're much less likely to find yourself on a different page from God if you allow His Word to guide your words.

> the bible reveals god's heart, what he wants for us—and from us.

The psalmists knew how important God's Word was to their prayers. Psalm 119, the longest chapter in the entire Bible, is practically a textbook example of how to use Scripture in communicating with God.

Check out these highlights:

Teach me, O LORD, the way of Your statutes,
And I shall keep it to the end.
Give me understanding, and I shall keep Your law;

Indeed, I shall observe it with my whole heart.
Make me walk in the path of Your commandments,
For I delight in it.
Incline my heart to Your testimonies,
And not to covetousness.
Turn away my eyes from looking at worthless things,
And revive me in Your way.
Establish Your word to Your servant,
Who is devoted to fearing You.
Turn away my reproach which I dread,
For Your judgments are good.
Behold, I long for Your precepts;
Revive me in Your righteousness . . .
Oh, how I love Your law!
It is my meditation all the day.
You, through Your commandments,
    make me wiser than my enemies;
For they are ever with me.
I have more understanding than all my teachers,
For Your testimonies are my meditation.
I understand more than the ancients,
Because I keep Your precepts.
I have restrained my feet from every evil way,
That I may keep Your word.
I have not departed from Your judgments,
For You Yourself have taught me.
How sweet are Your words to my taste,
Sweeter than honey to my mouth!
Through Your precepts I get understanding;
Therefore I hate every false way.

Your word is a lamp to my feet
And a light to my path. (Ps. 119:33–40, 97–105)

The psalmist brought everything back to God's Word. It's as if the Bible was his secret weapon for developing an extreme relationship with the Lord. It can be yours too. To have a creative change of pace, you could use portions of Psalm 119, word for word, in your own prayers.

Some classic lines in the passage you just read would sound great in any conversation with God. Here are just a few examples:

"incline my heart to your testimonies"

Think of this as tuning in to a radio station. It's like asking God to hit the right preset button on your heart so that it picks up His Word clearly. If you're tuned in to the Bible, anything else that tries to come through your "frequency"—whether it's temptation, doubt, or whatever—is going to seem a little staticky and distant. More important, though, it won't be able to capture your full attention.

"turn away my eyes from looking at worthless things"

This is how praying God's Word leads to spiritual growth. When you learn to focus on what's important—namely, your relationship with the Lord and His Word—an added benefit is that you learn to recognize worthless (and spiritually dangerous) things pretty quickly. The more time you spend locked in on Scripture and talking to God about it, the less time you have to worry about getting sidetracked from the spiritual journey.

HEADS UP

Knowing God's Word

God's Word is so powerful that even Jesus used it as His defense. In Luke 4:1–13, Jesus and Satan faced off in the desert. Satan tempted Jesus in every creative and sneaky way he could devise. It went something like this:

Satan said, "Jesus, you haven't eaten in forty days. Just make these stones bread."

Jesus replied, "Forget it. The Bible says that I don't just live by bread—I live off the word of God."

Satan said, "If you bow to me, I'll give you all the kingdoms on earth."

Jesus replied, "Back off, Satan! The Bible says to worship God only. Period."

Satan tried again. "Well, throw yourself off the temple and let the angels catch you."

Jesus replied, "Enough! The Bible says never to tempt God."

Because Jesus knew the Scriptures so well, He didn't say, "Now where was that verse that I read about . . . ?" He just whipped it off the top of His head. Knowing the Bible can transform your spiritual life and particularly your prayer life.

"your law . . . is my meditation all the day"

Nobody expects you to have your nose in a Bible 24/7. That's not what this verse is saying. The idea here is that

God's Word is always in your mind, even when you're not studying. Developing that kind of stamina takes practice. You'll need to learn how to refresh yourself by finding ways to apply specific verses and passages to your everyday life.

"how sweet are your words to my taste"

This isn't just nice talk, the kind of compliment you'd give someone on a first date. This is the psalmist's way of saying, "You know what, God? Your Word is like a special treat to me." You know how your mouth waters and your stomach growls when you see something sweet that you want to eat? That's the reaction God's looking for when it comes to His Word. He wants you to crave it.

Obviously, to be able to pray back sections of Scripture with sincerity, you have to be committed to studying God's Word. Don't take it lightly. God has loaded His Book with more wisdom, truth, direction, and comfort than you could find in a lifetime of study. He expects you to uncover as much of it as possible. The good news is that with serious Bible study, you can find something new and amazing about God's Word every day of your life.

Even better, not only do you have access to this incredible book, but you also have 24/7 access to the Author. So when you run across something in your Bible study that bothers you, you have the option of turning to God and saying,

- ◉ "I just don't get this, Lord. Help me understand what it means."
- ◉ "This is so cool. Thank You for caring about me."

● "I'm having a hard time dealing with this right now, Lord. Please give me strength."

Remember, this is God's heart we're talking about. He's going to be all over any prayer requests that deal with His Word. The Bible was written out of God's love for us. He didn't want us to be ignorant when it came to His will, so He told us everything we need to know.

> sin is a slap
> in the face to God.

When you pray God's Word back to Him, you claim the promises He's given you. It's also a way of showing your appreciation and love for the Bible.

What's it to You?

If you commit yourself to making God's Word part of your prayer life, then you can look forward to all kinds of spiritual benefits. Let's discuss a few of them.

forgiveness

Remember, you can't expect to grow spiritually if you have unconfessed sin in your life. It's that simple.

Let's say you and your best friend get in an argument, and in the heat of the moment, you smack your friend right across the face and walk out. Are you going to be able to go to that friend the next day and act as though everything's cool, as though nothing ever happened? No way. Your friend's not going to forget a shot to the face. You're going to have to do some serious apologizing to make things right.

Well, sin is a slap in the face to God. So when you sin, you can't expect things to be cool between you and Him until you apologize and make a real effort to change.

Again, enter God's Word. Not only is the Bible the place to go to learn God's will and His laws, and not only is it crammed full of reminders to repent, but it also contains real-life stories and prayers of people who went to God for forgiveness. The examples can come in handy when you're facing a similar situation.

Check out this one, for example:

Good and upright is the LORD;
Therefore He teaches sinners in the way.
The humble He guides in justice,
And the humble He teaches His way.
All the paths of the LORD are mercy and truth,
To such as keep His covenant and His testimonies.
For Your name's sake, O LORD,
Pardon my iniquity, for it is great.
Who is the man that fears the LORD?
Him shall He teach in the way He chooses.
He himself shall dwell in prosperity,
And his descendants shall inherit the earth.
The secret of the LORD is with those who fear Him,
And He will show them His covenant.
My eyes are ever toward the LORD,
For He shall pluck my feet out of the net.
Turn Yourself to me, and have mercy on me,
For I am desolate and afflicted.

The troubles of my heart have enlarged;
Bring me out of my distresses!
Look on my affliction and my pain,
And forgive all my sins.
Consider my enemies, for they are many;
And they hate me with cruel hatred.
Keep my soul, and deliver me;
Let me not be ashamed, for I put my trust in You.
Let integrity and uprightness preserve me,
For I wait for You. (Ps. 25:8–21)

This is the kind of thing you want to hear from someone who knows what he's talking about. David, the author of the psalm, was describing his experience with the Lord. He was saying, "If you come to the Lord in a humble way, admitting that you've done wrong, He will take care of you."

Here's what's really cool, though. If David's words sound good to you, you can pray them right back to God to claim His forgiveness, guidance, and protection. They worked for David, and they'll work for you. If you're uncomfortable with praying words such as *iniquity, desolate,* and *uprightness,* change them to fit your vocabulary. Or you could just use David's prayer as a general guideline for your own prayer of forgiveness. Whatever you choose to do, you can't go wrong with using Scripture in your prayers.

Remember, praying for forgiveness clears the way for all other spiritual growth. Once you've eliminated the obstacles to your relationship with the Lord, you can move on to other areas of spiritual growth.

Wisdom

Never underestimate wisdom. When David's son Solomon became king of Israel, he sacrificed a thousand burnt offerings to show his dedication to the Lord. After his offering, God appeared to Solomon and said, "Ask! What shall I give you?"

It was an open-request line. Basically God told Solomon, "Name one thing you want, and it's yours." Imagine the possibilities:

- Unbelievable riches
- Worldwide fame
- Long life and perfect health
- A prime parking spot right in front of the palace

Solomon could have asked for any of those things. Here's the answer he came up with:

> Now, O LORD my God, You have made Your servant king instead of my father David, but I am a little child; I do not know how to go out or come in. And Your servant is in the midst of Your people whom You have chosen, a great people, too numerous to be numbered or counted. Therefore give to Your servant an understanding heart to judge Your people, that I may discern between good and evil. For who is able to judge this great people of Yours? (1 Kings 3:7–9)

I'll take wisdom, Solomon decided.

Good choice, dude. God was pleased with Solomon's decision and responded:

Because you have asked this thing, and have not asked long life for yourself, nor have asked riches for yourself, nor have asked the life of your enemies, but have asked for yourself understanding to discern justice, behold, I have done according to your words; see, I have given you a wise and understanding heart, so that there has not been anyone like you before you, nor shall any like you arise after you. And I have also given you what you have not asked: both riches and honor, so that there shall not be anyone like you among the kings all your days. So if you walk in My ways, to keep My statutes and My commandments, as your father David walked, then I will lengthen your days. (1 Kings 3:11–14)

Ding! Ding! Ding! You can almost hear the bells and whistles going off and see the confetti falling. Solomon won the grand prize with that answer. He received riches, fame, long life—all in addition to the wisdom he asked for. He scored big time because his number one priority was God's number one priority. What does that say to you about how God feels about wisdom?

Now, you're not guaranteed riches, fame, or long life, but if you're interested in the same kind of wisdom that Solomon asked for—that is, the ability to make God-honoring decisions in your everyday situations—you can have it.

One of the first steps in gaining that kind of wisdom is recognizing how much you need it. Solomon called himself "a little child," referring to how little he really knew compared to what God had to offer. He approached God with a humble spirit and said, "I need You to show me what I need to know."

That's the same approach you need to take when you ask God for wisdom. It's not a onetime deal where you ask God for it and—*bam!*—suddenly you're wise. Wisdom comes in bits and pieces. It's a matter of praying for God's guidance, learning from your experiences, and studying His Word.

David asked God for wisdom in this prayer:

Show me Your ways, O LORD;
Teach me Your paths.
Lead me in Your truth and teach me,
For You are the God of my salvation;
On You I wait all the day. (Ps. 25:4–5)

Notice he didn't say, "Make me smart, Lord." He wasn't looking for a brain transplant. He used words such as *show* and *teach*. David recognized that becoming wise was a learning process. Each time he went back to the Lord in prayer, each time he studied God's Word, he learned a little more.

That's one of the things that kept David going back to God in prayer. And when you get a taste of the kind of wisdom he and Solomon were seeking, it will keep you coming back too.

loving heart

In Chapter 6, we talked about intercession, praying for other people. As far as God's concerned, that's not where our responsibilities end. The more spiritually mature you become, the more you'll recognize the importance of actually getting involved in other people's lives. As we learned, our prayers will evolve from "God, help them," to "God, show me how to help them."

It's not necessarily an instinct you're born with. The fact is, below the surface, most of us are pretty self-centered. And that's where prayer comes in. God can change your heart and the way you regard your responsibilities to other people—if you ask.

The apostle Paul did a nice job of laying out our responsibilities to others and giving us an idea of what to pray for in his letter to the Colossians:

> As the elect of God, holy and beloved, put on tender mercies, kindness, humility, meekness, longsuffering; bearing with one another, and forgiving one another, if anyone has a complaint against another; even as Christ forgave you, so you also must do. But above all these things put on love, which is the bond of perfection. And let the peace of God rule in your hearts, to which also you were called in one body; and be thankful. Let the word of Christ dwell in you richly in all wisdom, teaching and admonishing one another in psalms and hymns and spiritual songs, singing with grace in your hearts to the Lord. And whatever you do in word or deed, do all in the name of the Lord Jesus, giving thanks to God the Father through Him. (Col. 3:12–17)

Christians from Paul's day until now have struggled with these expectations. The wise ones have turned to the Lord for help. We can definitely learn from them too:

O Lord, give us more charity, more self-denial, more likeness to you. Teach us to sacrifice our comforts to others and our likings for the sake of doing good. Make us kindly in thought, gentle in word, generous in deed. Teach us that it is better to give than to receive, better to forget ourselves than to put ourselves forward, better to minister than to be ministered unto. And to you, the God of Love, be all glory and praise, now and forever. (Henry Alford, 1810–71)

Equip me today, O God, with
The humility which will keep me
    from pride and from conceit;
The graciousness and the gentleness
    which will make me
both easy to live with and a joy to meet;
The diligence, the perseverance, and the reliability
    which will make me a good workman;
The kindness which will give me a quick eye
to see what I can do for others,
and a ready hand to do it;
The constant awareness of your presence,
    which will make me
do everything as unto you.
So grant that today people may see in me
    a glimpse of the life of my blessed Lord.
This I ask for your love's sake. Amen.
        (William Barclay, 1907–78)

It's obvious that these writers were really trying to have loving hearts. And if you approach God in the same way, He will honor your requests and open your heart toward others.

one last thing

Spiritual growth is an individual thing. No official timetables, no schedules, no growth charts. And you absolutely cannot compare your spiritual life to the lives of the people you know. Everyone's relationship with the Lord is unique. Besides, when you focus on where other people are, you lose sight of your calling. All you need to know is that consistent, genuine prayer and Bible study always produce spiritual growth.

taking it to heart

Time to put the ol' gray matter to work. The path to spiritual growth can be rocky. Navigating it successfully takes a lot of work, perseverance, and discipline. To help prepare you for the process, consider the following questions. If an extreme prayer life is your goal, you'll need to put some time and thought into your answers.

1. What area of your spiritual life is in need of growth right now? Why do you think that is?
2. Have you ever noticed spiritual growth in other people? If so, what did you notice?
3. Have others ever noticed spiritual growth in you? If so, what did they notice?

4. How do you feel about making God's Word part of your prayers? What benefits do you think you'll see? What drawbacks do you think you might experience?

5. Think about the last time you prayed for forgiveness. What words did you use? How did you feel afterward? What changes, if any, will you make the next time you pray for forgiveness?

6. If you had the kind of wisdom Solomon prayed for, how would it affect your life?

7. Name three steps you can take to develop a more loving heart toward others.

One from the heart

Based on what you've learned about spiritual growth in this chapter, write your own prayer to God. Try to focus on one area in which you'd like to see growth. And try to be as specific as possible throughout your prayer.

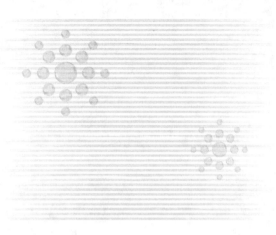

9

SHHH, LISTEN!

One night David was hanging out on his roof when something caught his eye. He noticed a beautiful woman taking a bath on a nearby roof. He did a double take and then kept staring. This babe was hot! She had it going on, and she wasn't wearing too much. David was interested, to say the least. In fact, he was so interested that he sent one of his servants to find out who she was.

David wanted Bathsheba. He found out that she was married to a guy named Uriah, who just happened to be one of David's best soldiers. Since Uriah was away fighting a battle (for the king), David invited Bathsheba over to his place. For the night. Like a sleepover, and they slept together. The result? Bathsheba got pregnant.

Major problem for David. With Uriah out of town, it wouldn't take long for people to put it together that this was not Uriah's child. David had a crisis on his hands, and he had no time to fix it.

So he came up with a plan. He ordered one of his generals to send Uriah home from the battle. David was thinking that if Uriah slept with his wife while he was home, then everyone would assume that Uriah had fathered the baby.

David didn't count on Uriah's extreme dedication to his fellow soldiers. When Uriah got back to Jerusalem, he didn't go home, as David had hoped. Instead, he slept outside David's door, just waiting to be sent back to battle.

So David tried again. This time he invited Uriah to a nice dinner and got him drunk. He figured that if Uriah was wasted, he'd be more likely to go home and sleep with his wife. But Uriah didn't budge. Again he slept in front of David's door, waiting to be sent back to battle. What a noble man. What a striking contrast.

David was desperate. He couldn't let the truth get out. He wrote a letter to one of his generals, instructing him to put Uriah on the front line of the battle and then secretly pull back the rest of the troops, leaving Uriah alone to fight the enemy. The general obeyed David's brutal command, and Uriah was killed in battle.

(In case you're wondering, this is the David we're talking about—the same guy who killed Goliath, became king of Israel, wrote a big chunk of the book of Psalms, and was called "the man after God's own heart." Lying, adultery, murder—when this guy messed up, he really messed up.)

When Bathsheba found out that her husband was dead, she mourned for him for seven days. Then she moved into David's house and became his wife. A little less than nine months later, she gave birth to a baby boy. David figured that since Bathsheba was officially his wife, no one would know the truth about when the baby was conceived.

David was wrong. God knew the truth. He always knows. And He wasn't happy about it. So God sent the prophet Nathan to let

David know that He knew the truth. Nathan confronted David about his sin, then told him that his newborn son would die.

As you might expect, David lost it when he heard Nathan's words. All the months of pent-up guilt, shame, and anxiety broke, and he completely fell apart. You can find evidence of his intense emotions in Psalm 51, which David wrote in the midst of this crisis. (Remember this from Chapter 1?) Take a glimpse at his emotions:

> To the Chief Musician. A Psalm of David when Nathan the prophet went to him, after he had gone in to Bathsheba.
>
> Have mercy upon me, O God,
> According to Your lovingkindness;
> According to the multitude of Your tender mercies,
> Blot out my transgressions.
> Wash me thoroughly from my iniquity,
> And cleanse me from my sin.
> For I acknowledge my transgressions,
> And my sin is always before me.
> Against You, You only, have I sinned,
> And done this evil in Your sight—
> That You may be found just when You speak,
> And blameless when You judge. (Ps. 51:1–4)

For seven days David put his life on hold and devoted every moment to praying for his newborn son. He spent his days and nights lying on the ground, begging God to spare his child's life. He refused all food and comfort for an entire week as he poured out his deepest feelings to his heavenly Father.

And at the end of the seven days . . . the baby died.
Whoa.

it's like this

Our first reaction might be to wonder why God didn't answer David's desperate prayers to spare his son's life. The fact is, God did answer David's prayers. He said no.

> sometimes his ways are too mysterious for our human brains to comprehend.

We could spend the rest of this book trying to figure out why God said no, but it would be a waste of time and space. What it all comes down to is this: God is much too complex for us to figure out. Sometimes His ways are too mysterious for our human brains to comprehend.

A better approach for us would be to explore David's reaction to the situation:

> When David saw that his servants were whispering, David perceived that the child was dead. Therefore David said to his servants, "Is the child dead?" And they said, "He is dead." So David arose from the ground, washed and anointed himself, and changed his clothes; and he went into the house of the LORD and worshiped. Then he went to his own house; and when he requested, they set food before him, and he ate. Then his servants said to him, "What is this that you have done? You fasted and wept for the child while he was alive, but

when the child died, you arose and ate food." And he
said, "While the child was alive, I fasted and wept; for I
said, 'Who can tell whether the LORD will be gracious to
me, that the child may live?' But now he is dead; why
should I fast? Can I bring him back again? I shall go to
him, but he shall not return to me." (2 Sam. 12:19–23)

Does David's response seem weird to you? When you
think about it, it shouldn't. While his child was alive, David
still had a legitimate prayer: "Please don't let my child die."
When God answered his prayer, it might not have been the
solution David wanted, but it was an answer.

And once he had his answer, David was able to get on
with the grieving process and, eventually, the rest of his life.

We want to examine how David was able to react the way
he did.

Word

Let's clarify one thing now, so there's no confusion. God
answers prayer. The Bible is very clear about that fact:

Ask, and it will be given to you; seek, and you will
find; knock, and it will be opened to you. For everyone
who asks receives, and he who seeks finds, and to him
who knocks it will be opened. Or what man is there
among you who, if his son asks for bread, will give him
a stone? Or if he asks for a fish, will he give him a serpent? If you then, being evil, know how to give good
gifts to your children, how much more will your Father

who is in heaven give good things to those who ask Him! (Matt. 7:7–11)

You are My friends if you do whatever I command you. No longer do I call you servants, for a servant does not know what his master is doing; but I have called you friends, for all things that I heard from My Father I have made known to you. You did not choose Me, but I chose you and appointed you that you should go and bear fruit, and that your fruit should remain, that whatever you ask the Father in My name He may give you. These things I command you, that you love one another. (John 15:14–17)

Now this is the confidence that we have in Him, that if we ask anything according to His will, He hears us. And if we know that He hears us, whatever we ask, we know that we have the petitions that we have asked of Him. (1 John 5:14–15)

These are all inspiring, heartwarming, and encouraging passages, especially when God is answering your prayers in an obvious way. But when it seems that you're not getting any response from Him, you may chime in with David when he asked,

How long, O LORD? Will You forget me forever?
How long will You hide Your face from me? (Ps. 13:1)

Even with all of the biblical assurance available, life can be pretty frustrating when it seems that you're being ignored by God. That's where faith and silence come in handy.

Faith is necessary because you must believe that God answers all prayers. Sometimes He answers, "Yes." Sometimes He answers, "No." Sometimes He answers, "Not yet." But He always answers. It's also important to believe that God's "no" and "not yet" responses are ultimately just as beneficial to us as His yeses. We have to

> faith is necessary because you must believe that God answers all prayers.

learn to cling to the promise of Romans 8:28: "We know that all things work together for good to those who love God, to those who are the called according to His purpose."

→ **HEADS UP**

Getting a "yes" response from God has nothing to do with who you are or how spiritual you are. Paul, for example, would likely finish in the top five Christians of all time.

But consider what he said about his prayer life in 2 Corinthians 12:7–10:

Lest I should be exalted above measure by the abundance of the revelations, a thorn in the flesh was given to me, a messenger of Satan to buffet me, lest I be exalted above measure. Concerning this thing I pleaded with the Lord three times that it might depart from me. And He said to me, "My grace is sufficient for you, for

My strength is made perfect in weakness." Therefore
most gladly I will rather boast in my infirmities, that the
power of Christ may rest upon me. Therefore I take
pleasure in infirmities, in reproaches, in needs, in perse-
cutions, in distresses, for Christ's sake. For when I am
weak, then I am strong.

Many people think Paul's "thorn in the flesh" was an eye
problem. Perhaps he even had problems seeing. Whatever the
affliction was, Paul prayed to be healed of it. And God said . . .
"No." He wanted Paul to rely on Him for his strength. He also
wanted people to recognize His work in Paul's life.

What often happens, though, is that people fail to recognize God's "no" or "not yet" responses and they assume that
He's not listening to them or not answering them for some
reason. To put it another way, some people confuse not getting what they want with not having their prayers answered.

The Bible is clear about what you need to do to hear
God's answers (whatever they may be) to your prayers:

The LORD called Samuel again the third time. Then
he arose and went to Eli, and said, "Here I am, for you
did call me." Then Eli perceived that the LORD had
called the boy. Therefore Eli said to Samuel, "Go, lie
down; and it shall be, if He calls you, that you must say,
'Speak, LORD, for Your servant hears.'" So Samuel went
and lay down in his place. (1 Sam. 3:8–9)

Be still, and know that I am God;
I will be exalted among the nations,
I will be exalted in the earth! (Ps. 46:10)

I will stand my watch
And set myself on the rampart,
And watch to see what He will say to me,
And what I will answer when I am corrected. (Hab. 2:1)

Look closely at the phrases "Your servant hears"; "Be still"; and "Watch to see what He will say." Obviously the key to recognizing answered prayers is keeping your eyes and ears open.

But what are you looking and listening for? How do you recognize an answer to prayer? What does God's voice sound like? Elijah, one of the heroes of the Bible, wondered the same thing. The answer he got was surprising, to say the least.

> [God said to Elijah,] "Go out, and stand on the mountain before the LORD." And behold, the LORD passed by, and a great and strong wind tore into the mountains and broke the rocks in pieces before the LORD, but the LORD was not in the wind; and after the wind an earth-quake, but the LORD was not in the earthquake; and after the earthquake a fire, but the LORD was not in the fire; and after the fire a still small voice. (1 Kings 19:11–12)

God could have come to Elijah in a strong wind, an earth-quake, or a fire. But that's not the way He chose to work.

Instead, He chose to speak in a still small voice that Elijah had to listen carefully to hear.

You can learn a lot about prayer from Elijah's experience. If you're expecting God to be all in your face with a spectacular answer to your prayers, you may miss His still small voice. So learn to listen.

Christians from the time of Jesus until today have recognized the importance of quiet times and listening. Many of them have turned to God for help. Check out these historical prayers:

O Lord, my God,
grant us your peace; already, indeed,
    you have made us rich in all things!
Give us that peace of being at rest,
that sabbath peace,
the peace which knows no end. (Saint Augustine, 354–430)

O Lord, the Scripture says "there is a time for silence and a time for speech." Savior, teach me the silence of humility, the silence of wisdom, the silence of love, the silence of perfection, the silence that speaks without words, the silence of faith.

Lord, teach me to silence my own heart that I may listen to the gentle movement of the Holy Spirit within me and sense the depths which are of God. (Frankfurt Prayer, sixteenth century)

Dear Lord and Father of mankind,
Forgive our foolish ways!

Reclothe us in our rightful mind;
In purer lives your service find,
In deeper reverence, praise.
Drop your still dews of quietness
Till all our strivings cease:
Take from our lives the strain and stress,
And let our ordered lives confess
The beauty of your peace. (John Greenleaf Whittier, 1807–92)

Give unto us, O Lord, that quietness of mind
  in which we can hear you speaking to us,
   for your own name's sake.
Lord, you have taught us in your word
  that there is a time to speak
and a time to keep silence.
As we thank you for the power of speech,
we pray for the grace of silence.
Make us as ready to listen as we are to talk,
ready to listen to your voice in the quietness of our hearts
and ready to listen to other people
  who need a sympathetic ear.
Show us when to open our mouths and when
  to hold our peace
that we may glorify you both in speech and in silence
through Jesus Christ our Lord. (Frank Colquhoun)

To be there before you, Lord, that's all.
To shut the eyes of my body,
To shut the eyes of my soul,
And be still and silent,

To expose myself to you who are there, exposed to me.
To be there before you, the Eternal Presence. (Michael Quoist)

Once you experience the kind of peace and quietness these Christians were seeking, your prayer life will be changed forever. You'll discover what it's like to have an actual dialogue with God.

What's it to You?

More often than not, God will respond to your prayer requests in low-key ways, using methods you may not have associated with prayer before. The tools He will use include these:

- Your conscience
- His Word
- Other people
- Circumstances

Let's take a closer look at each of them.

Your Conscience

Remember the "still small voice" that Elijah heard? Doesn't that description remind you of your conscience? Think about it. When you do something that you know goes against God's will, don't you hear a still small voice telling you that it's wrong?

Could God use that same voice to answer your prayers? Absolutely. For Christians, the Holy Spirit serves as our conscience. So it's His voice we hear when we do something wrong—and when we need guidance.

Have you ever faced a choice that somehow just seemed wrong to you? Maybe you couldn't put your finger on exactly what the problem was, but you still felt sure that it was wrong. Some people call it a gut instinct. You can call it your conscience at work.

For example, let's say you asked the Lord to bless your dating relationship. If you later experienced some guilt about the physical part of your relationship and started to doubt whether you were dating the right person or not, you could safely assume that the Lord was answering your prayer.

As early as the first century A.D., Christians recognized the importance of the Holy Spirit in revealing God's will. Check out the following prayer from that period:

> O Lord Almighty, Father of our Lord Jesus Christ, grant us, we pray thee, to be grounded and settled in thy truth by the coming down of the Holy Spirit into our hearts. That which we know not do thou reveal, that which is wanting in us do thou fill up, that which we know do thou confirm, and keep us blameless in thy service, through the same Jesus Christ our Lord. (Saint Clement of Rome)

One thing to keep in mind about the still small voice of your conscience is that the more you ignore it, the fainter it becomes. If you neglect it too long, you risk destroying it completely. You risk hardening your heart and severing your conscience. That's why it's important to always listen for the Holy Spirit's communication, no matter what you're doing.

God's Word

This is a tricky one, especially when you consider that some of the worst crimes in history have been committed by people who claimed they were inspired by the Bible. The sad truth is that you can justify just about anything with the Bible if you take enough verses out of context and ignore everything else in it.

And don't try that open-the-book-and-point-to-a-verse strategy, either. That's not the way God wants you to discover His wisdom and guidance. For the most part, the answers to prayer that God offers through His Word are part of a *committed* Bible study. If you're in God's Word on a regular basis, looking for ways to apply what you learn to your life, God will direct you to the passages you need when you need them.

For example, let's say you're having problems in your relationship with your mother, and you ask God to help you deal with it. He might direct your attention to Proverbs 31:10–31, which offers a description of an ideal woman, to help you appreciate your mom for all the things that she selflessly does for your family.

Other People

They're called mentors, and they're a vital part of the Christian life. They are mature Christians who are willing to share their wisdom and experience to help you avoid mistakes and make sound decisions.

When you're facing tough times, God may bring mentors into your life to give you advice and direction. A mentor may be someone like a youth leader, a pastor, or a parent. The only criteria are that the mentor should have a godly perspective on life, a concern for your best interests, and a willingness to confront you whenever necessary.

For example, let's say you have a habit you're trying to kick and you ask the Lord for His help. In response, God may bring someone into your life

> the harder you look for evidence of answered prayer, the better chance you'll have of seeing him at work.

who struggled with and overcame a similar habit. The person can share personal experiences to make your life easier and your efforts more effective. And that person can help hold you accountable to live up to God's calling on your life.

Circumstances

God may also choose to shut some doors in your life and open others to make sure that you end up where you need to be. The problem is that unless you're looking for those door openings and closings, you may not recognize them when they occur. And if you don't recognize them, you certainly won't pick up on the fact that they're answers to prayer.

For example, let's say that after praying for God to give you a better career opportunity than your current job does, you receive three great job offers within a week. Each offer has strengths and weaknesses, so you're really not sure which one is right for you. In that situation God may cause two of the offers to fall through, leaving you with one clear shot.

Obviously these are basic examples. Real-life prayer requests are rarely so simple or so cut-and-dried. But the harder you look for evidence of answered prayer, the better chance you'll have of seeing Him at work.

Certainly God isn't restricted to these four tools. He can use just about anything to answer your prayers. He is God, after all. That's why it's important to always keep your "prayer antennae" up so that you don't miss one of His answers.

one last thing

If you're looking for a guideline, try this: at least half of the time you spend in prayer should be devoted to silence. Now, don't assume it's the kind of silence that makes your mind wander and your eyelids droop, though. It's the kind of silence during which you block out everything else and concentrate solely on listening to God.

You could spend part of that time searching your conscience, listening for God's still small voice speaking to you about a situation in your life. You could spend part of it reading Scripture, giving God an opportunity to speak to you that way. You could spend part of it thinking about the advice of trusted Christian friends. You could spend part of it reviewing recent events in your life, trying to identify any doors that have been opened or closed.

However you choose to spend your quiet time, treat it just as seriously as you do the verbal part of your prayers. Extreme prayer is not possible without an extreme quiet time.

taking it to heart

Time to put the ol' gray matter to work. Learning to hear God's voice and recognize His answers to prayer takes a lot of practice. To help prepare for what's ahead, answer the following questions. If a passionate prayer life is your goal, you'll need to put some time and thought into your answers.

1. When was the last time God answered "yes" to one of your prayer requests? How did you recognize it as an answer to prayer?

2. When was the last time God answered "no" to one of your prayer requests? How did you recognize it as an answer to prayer?

3. Write down a situation in which God might say "not yet" to a prayer request.

4. Why is listening in prayer such a difficult habit to master?

5. What steps can you take to improve your listening skills when it comes to prayer?

6. Write down a situation in which God may have used your conscience to give you direction in life.

7. Write down a situation in which God may have used His Word to give you direction in life.

8. Write down a situation in which God may have used other people to give you direction in life.

9. Write down a situation in which God may have opened and closed doors in your life to give you direction.

one from the heart

Based on what you've learned about listening and waiting for God's response in this chapter, write your own prayer
to God. Try to focus on the receiving end of prayer—how you
can become a better listener. And try to be as specific as possible throughout your prayer.

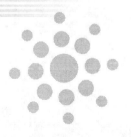

10
INTERFERENCE!

Prayer is like a New Year's resolution for me. I always start out with really good intentions, but then something happens. I make plans to start praying once a day, but then I end up praying, like, once a month or something. It's kind of pathetic, actually. I don't know what happens to me.

—*Kelly, age twenty-two*

☀ ☀ ☀

My problem is that the only time I have to pray is just before bed, when I'm completely wiped out from the day. No matter what I do to try to stay awake, I can't seem to get through a whole prayer without falling asleep. I know it's not the best way to pray, but what else can I do?

—*Tracy, age twenty-four*

*If I don't feel close to God, I have a hard time praying. It feels
fake to me, you know what I'm saying? I feel like I'm pretending
sometimes because the words I'm saying don't match the way I'm
feeling. So usually I just say a few things, maybe the Lord's Prayer
or something, and then hope that I'll feel closer to God next time.*

—Martin, age nineteen

it's like this

If you decide to become an extreme pray-er, you can count
on this: not everyone's going to be happy about your decision.
In fact, a certain someone is going to be quite upset about it—
so upset that he's going to do whatever he can to spoil your
plans: "Be sober, be vigilant; because your adversary the devil
walks about like a roaring lion, seeking whom he may devour"
(1 Peter 5:8).

Satan's no fool. He knows that prayer is your lifeline to
God. He also knows that if he can interfere with that connection, he has a good chance of stalling your spiritual growth.

Of course, if a roaring lion was all you had to look out for,
you might be okay. At least you'd be able to see it coming. But
a lion is not the only disguise Satan wears. And fear and
intimidation are not the only strategies he uses. He's also
pretty good at recognizing your most vulnerable points and
taking full advantage of them. That's probably the method
he'll use when he attacks your prayer life.

Word

Fortunately, God's Word has quite a bit to say about Satan

and his ways. After all, understanding your enemy is the key to defeating him:

> Finally, my brethren, be strong in the Lord and in the power of His might. Put on the whole armor of God, that you may be able to stand against the wiles of the devil. For we do not wrestle against flesh and blood, but against principalities, against powers, against the rulers of the darkness of this age, against spiritual hosts of wickedness in the heavenly places. Therefore take up the whole armor of God, that you may be able to withstand in the evil day, and having done all, to stand. Stand therefore, having girded your waist with truth, having put on the breastplate of righteousness, and having shod your feet with the preparation of the gospel of peace; above all, taking the shield of faith with which you will be able to quench all the fiery darts of the wicked one. And take the helmet of salvation, and the sword of the Spirit, which is the word of God; praying always with all prayer and supplication in the Spirit, being watchful to this end with all perseverance and supplication for all the saints—and for me, that utterance may be given to me, that I may open my mouth boldly to make known the mystery of the gospel, for which I am an ambassador in chains; that in it I may speak boldly, as I ought to speak. (Eph. 6:10–20)

Satan has had thousands of years to perfect his battle strategies. He's pretty good at what he does. When he throws everything he has at you, you'd better be ready for it, or you're in trouble.

What's it to You?

The best way to protect yourself from Satan's schemes is to prepare for them. To help you prepare, we're going to identify eight obstacles he may use to interfere with your prayer life. We'll also look at a few basic strategies for overcoming each one.

Obstacle #1: busyness

Get a load of this nugget of advice from William Penn (1644–1718): "In the rush and noise of life, as you have intervals, step within yourselves and be still. Wait upon God and feel his good presence; this will carry you through your day's business."

If dear old Penn thought life was rushed and noisy at the turn of the eighteenth century, how do you think he'd feel about life in the twenty-first century? You live in the fastest, busiest, and most chaotic time in human history. You have more responsibilities, opportunities, and diversions competing for your attention than the people of Mr. Penn's day ever dreamed possible.

If Penn thought it was difficult to maintain a regular prayer life in horse-and-buggy days, what chance do you have in a world of seventy-hour workweeks, satellite television, and instant Internet access?

Actually you have a very good chance of maintaining an extreme prayer life if you learn to give it the priority it deserves.

The key is to treat your prayer time like a scheduled

appointment. You wouldn't dream of blowing off a meeting with your boss or an important job interview just to watch TV or play a few video games. (Okay, maybe you'd dream about it, but you wouldn't actually do it.) That same attitude should apply to your prayer life.

If you use a daily organizer, block out a time each day for a fifteen-minute (or however long) meeting with God. And make that appointment nonnegotiable. If something else comes up at the last minute, find another time to deal with it. Don't sacrifice your prayer time.

Nothing is more important than your daily meeting with God, so nothing should ever interfere with it—not work or play or even a date. Nothing. Regardless of how crazy things get in your life or how jammed your schedule becomes, it's absolutely important that you keep your appointment with God every day.

Obstacle #2: Complacency

This is one of Satan's slickest strategies for messing up a healthy prayer life. He lulls you into thinking that things are so good in your life that there's no need for prayer. You figure you'll just wait until something happens and you really need God's help before you pray. It's the same type of thinking that makes people say, "I don't need a dental checkup. My teeth feel fine."

The first problem with this way of thinking is that it treats prayer as something you do on an "as needed" basis. And that's not what prayer is about at all. Prayer isn't an emergency procedure or a last resort when all else fails; it's a way of drawing a little closer to God every day through one-on-one conversation. Every prayer time you blow off is a missed opportunity to get to know God—and His will for your life—a little better. That should inspire you to hit your knees on a regular basis. Remember, this is the Creator of the universe we're talking about.

The second problem with this way of thinking is that it causes you to believe that the status quo is good. The truth is, there is no status quo where your spiritual life is concerned. If you're not growing a little every day in your spiritual life, you're losing ground. The minute you start to feel self-satisfied with where you are, you fall a little behind.

> if you're not growing a little every day in your spiritual life, you're losing ground.

Keep this in mind: no matter how much you grow spiritually, you will never outgrow your need for prayer. In fact, just the opposite is true. The more you grow spiritually, the more important prayer will become to you. The hunger to get to know God better should never go away.

obstacle #3: doubt

We talked about doubt in detail earlier in this book, so this is just a reminder of how it can become a major obstacle to an extreme prayer life.

Hear what James, the New Testament author, had to say about doubt:

> My brethren, count it all joy when you fall into various trials, knowing that the testing of your faith pro-

duces patience. But let patience have its perfect work, that you may be perfect and complete, lacking nothing. If any of you lacks wisdom, let him ask of God, who gives to all liberally and without reproach, and it will be given to him. But let him ask in faith, with no doubting, for he who doubts is like a wave of the sea driven and tossed by the wind. For let not that man suppose that he will receive anything from the Lord; he is a double-minded man, unstable in all his ways. (James 1:2–8)

James wasn't talking about the kind of momentary doubts we all experience at one time or another. He wasn't talking about those fleeting feelings that caused David to write,

My God, My God, why have You forsaken Me?
Why are You so far from helping Me,
And from the words of My groaning?
O My God, I cry in the daytime, but You do not hear;
And in the night season, and am not silent. (Ps. 22:1–2)

James was talking about the kind of deep-seated, long-term doubts that cause you to question whether God really knows what's best for you or whether He has the power to affect the things that happen to you. These doubts can cause serious damage to your prayer life.

The best way to protect yourself from such doubts is to always be open and honest with God about your feelings. If you've been devastated by the loss of a loved one, or if you've experienced something that made you question God's good-ness, love, or power, then it's important that you talk to Him about it. Spill your guts. He won't be mad; He'll probably find a way to show you how much He genuinely loves and cares about you.

Obstacle #4: ignorance

First things first: we're not talking about a lack of intelli-gence here. There is no minimum IQ required to talk to God. (If there were, the author of this book would be in serious trouble.) What we're talking about is a lack of on-the-job experience.

If the idea of passionate prayer—or any kind of prayer—is new to you, you may be a little unsure about how to get started. That's only natural. Unfortunately, though, that uncertainty also gives Satan a prime place to attack your prayer life before it even gets started. He'll plant seeds of uncertainty in your mind.

Your best strategy for defending yourself against his attacks is perseverance. When you begin praying, you may feel a little intimidated, as if you're in over your head. You may be afraid of saying the wrong thing. Or you may feel really, really self-conscious.

There's nothing wrong with any of those feelings—at least, not when you first start praying. The key, though, is to get to the point that you're no longer intimidated by or uncomfortable with the idea of praying. And the best way to get to that point is to . . . well, pray. The more time you spend with God in prayer, the more confidence you'll gain in your ability to talk to Him one-on-one. And the more confidence you build, the less Satan will be able to use ignorance as an obstacle.

This is also where Christian mentors can help. If you're having problems starting a prayer time, talk to a mature believer about it. It might be someone in your family or church. Just make sure that the person you choose has enough experience as a Christian to help you. You may be surprised by what a difference another person's input can make in the way you approach prayer.

Whatever you do, though, don't let Satan use your inexperience or self-consciousness against you. Don't let him ruin what could be a Hall of Fame prayer career in your rookie season.

obstacle #5: indifference

Satan tries to take advantage of self-centeredness. If you struggle with self-centered tendencies from time to time . . . well, welcome to the human race. We all do. The problem comes when you allow self-centeredness to creep into your prayer life. When that happens, Satan pounces like the roaring lion that Peter compared him to (1 Peter 5:8).

In case you're wondering, a self-centered approach to prayer is focusing only on what affects *you* and *your* life. If Satan can make you indifferent to the needs of other people, he can rob your prayer life of most of its power. The idea of Christians lifting each other up in prayer is at the heart of fellowship. The idea of Christians lifting nonbelievers up in prayer is at the heart of evangelism. There's no avoiding intercession if you're after an extreme Christian life.

The apostle Paul certainly made a big deal about praying

for others. To the Christians in Rome, he wrote, "For God is my witness, whom I serve with my spirit in the gospel of His Son, that without ceasing I make mention of you always in my prayers" (Rom. 1:9).

To the Christians in Corinth, he wrote, "I thank my God always concerning you for the grace of God which was given to you by Christ Jesus" (1 Cor. 1:4).

Most of the letters that Paul wrote contain similar passages. It's obvious that he put his money where his mouth was when it came to intercession (praying for others).

The apostle John, though, really nailed our responsibility to others when he wrote,

> My little children, let us not love in word or in tongue, but in deed and in truth. And by this we know that we are of the truth, and shall assure our hearts before Him. For if our heart condemns us, God is greater than our heart, and knows all things. Beloved, if our heart does not condemn us, we have confidence toward God. And whatever we ask we receive from Him, because we keep His commandments and do those things that are pleasing in His sight. And this is His commandment: that we should believe on the name of His Son Jesus Christ and love one another, as He gave us commandment. (1 John 3:18–23)

That doesn't leave much room for self-centeredness, does it?

If a loving and concerned attitude toward others doesn't come naturally to you, don't beat yourself up about it. But don't let Satan take advantage of it, either. Instead, pray about it.

Ask God to

- make you more aware of the needs of others.
- help you develop meaningful prayer relationships with other Christians.
- give you a nudge whenever you drift toward self-centered prayer habits.

Let God smash the obstacle of indifference toward others before Satan has a chance to trip you up with it.

Obstacle #6: Jaziness

Laziness is probably the most common obstacle to a healthy prayer life. It's also the most despicable when you think about it.

For example, if Joey conveys through his words or actions, "I don't feel like praying today," he really means, "I don't feel like giving up the other things in my life that seem more interesting or important in order to talk to God." He's making prayer seem like a sacrifice or a hardship to him. And that's a complete joke.

If you want to talk about sacrifice or hardship, you've got to turn your attention to what God did to give Joey, and the rest of us, the privilege of praying to Him. You see, through Jesus is the only way we can get to God. God sacrificed His only Son—the only One who could pay the price for our sin—to reestablish the lines of contact with us. That's why people often end their prayers with the phrase

"In Jesus' name we pray." Any friend of Jesus is a friend of God.

When you allow laziness to keep you from enjoying the privilege of connecting with God in conversation, you're discounting the sacrifice that was necessary to make it possible. You're also making Satan's job a lot easier. If your laziness is enough to keep you out of prayer, he can just kick back and relax for a while.

This would be a good time to point out that the obstacles we're studying in this section are listed in alphabetical order, not in their order of importance. If you're looking for an obstacle to get rid of first, definitely attack this one. Allowing laziness to keep you from a healthy prayer life is about as blatant an insult to God as you can give.

The point is not what you have to give up to pray; the point is what God had to give up so that you would be able to pray.

Let's go over it one more time, just to make sure you have the complete picture. To open the lines of communication between you and Him, God allowed His Son to pay the ultimate price—a price that included His torture and murder. Consider that the next time you're tempted to moan about how hard it is to pray.

→ **HEADS UP**

Scheduled Appointment

Ever since he was young, Daniel set aside time every day to pray. In fact, we read in Daniel 6:10 that he had a routine. Three times each day, Daniel would open his window toward

Jerusalem, kneel down, and pray and give thanks to God. Since Daniel knew the importance of prayer, he made it a regular habit. He was willing to risk anything—even being fed to the lions—in order to keep his appointments with God.

Watch and Pray

Peter, James, and John were tight with Jesus. Yet, they failed Jesus when He needed them most, and it hurt Him deeply. In Matthew 26:36–46, Jesus and the three disciples went to the Garden of Gethsemane. Jesus knew what awaited Him that very night—arrest, trial, torture, and death. He dreaded it.

So He asked His three best friends to pray for Him. "Watch and pray," He said. Then He walked a little farther and fell on His face to pray to God.

When He came back, He found all three asleep. Even after He woke them up, they fell asleep two more times. They missed an important opportunity for prayer. Will you be found sleeping when He comes to find you?

obstacle #7: poor setting

Have you ever tried to have a long, quiet, one-on-one prayer time with God

- on the beach at spring break?
- at a rock concert?
- in the middle of a serious argument with someone?
- on a roller coaster?
- during a frat party?

Probably not—at least, not for very long. Nothing spoils the intimacy of prayer faster than a couple of distractions. When you put yourself in a place of constant distractions, there's not much hope for quality one-on-one time with God.

Realtors will tell you that the three most important things to consider when you're looking for a house are location, location, location. The same principle applies to your prayer life. If you're serious about becoming an extreme pray-er, you have to find the right location in which to spend your prayer time.

First of all, the place you choose should be comfortable. And we're not just talking about physical comfort, either. Sure, a comfy chair or padded carpet (for kneeling) is a good thing to have. But you should also find a place where you feel free to communicate with God in whatever way you choose. If you're self-conscious about people seeing you pray, sing, or read Scripture out loud, find a place that gives you complete solitude.

Second, the place you choose should be free of distractions. The fewer options you have in your prayer area, the better. That means no TV, no computer, no stereo, no magazines, no phone, no pager, no nothing—except your Bible and any other prayer resources you want to use.

Third, the place you choose should put you in a prayerful spirit. If you're looking at a poster of a half-naked model or a WWF screen saver on your computer while you pray, you may find it tough to concentrate on what the Lord is saying to you. So you should do whatever decorating or renovating you can to make your prayer space work for you.

If candles relax you and make you forget about the tension of the day, load up your prayer area with candles. If you like to be surrounded by God's Word, jot down some of your favorite Bible verses on index cards and tack them up around your prayer area. Do whatever you can to create a place where you can go for uninterrupted, quality time with the Lord.

Obstacle #8: Unconfessed Sin

Scripture passages such as Psalm 103.12 ("As far as the east is from the west, so far has He removed our transgressions from us") and 1 John 1:9 ("If we confess our sins, He is faithful and just to forgive us our sins and to cleanse us from all unrighteousness") guarantee that if you genuinely confess your sins to God, He will forgive and forget them.

Until you ask for His forgiveness, though, your sins will get in the way of your prayers and interfere with your communication with God.

Think about a few of the reasons that might motivate you to come to God in prayer without confessing a sin:

- The sin is a habit that you can't—or don't want to—control.
- You're not really sorry about what you've done. (This is especially true where revenge is involved.)
- You underestimate how much God hates sin.

You need to correct these attitudes before you can make any serious attempt to become an extreme pray-er.

Fortunately, one prayer you can send up in the midst of your "sin blockade" is a request for God to help you recognize the seriousness of your sin and to show you what you stand to gain by confessing and repenting.

Keep in mind that when you remove the obstacle of unconfessed sin, you clear the way for all kinds of spiritual growth—not to mention a passionate prayer life.

one last thing

For every obstacle to prayer that we discussed, there are probably at least ten that we didn't. If that number doesn't concern you, it should. If you're striving to create an extreme prayer life for yourself, you've got to be prepared to fight distractions and obstacles every day.

Satan doesn't take vacations. He's going to keep throwing everything he has at you to screw up your prayer life. He knows that if he can interfere with your communication with God, he can do serious damage to your spiritual growth.

The good news is that if you remain close to God, Satan doesn't stand a chance. If you stay focused on your relationship with the Lord 24/7, then passionate prayer is within your reach.

taking it to heart

Time to put the ol' gray matter to work. Avoiding distractions in your prayer life is a never-ending responsibility. Becoming an extreme pray-er requires a truckload of dedication and perseverance. To help prepare for the challenges that lie ahead, think through the following questions. If an extreme prayer life is your goal, you'll need to put as much time and thought as possible into your answers.

1. Describe in detail your prayer patterns right now. How do you feel about your habits? Why?

2. Why do you think that a Christian's prayer life is one of Satan's prime targets for attack?

3. What changes could you make to your daily schedule in order to carve out a time for prayer every day? How hard would it be to make those changes? Would you be willing to do it? Why or why not?

4. What causes the kind of deep-seated doubt that can ruin a prayer life? How can you avoid that kind of doubt in your life?

5. Describe what your prayer area is like. What changes would you like to make to it?

6. Write down two or three obstacles to prayer that have tripped you up in the past. What happened? What were the results? How likely is it that you'll be tripped up by the same obstacles again? Why?

7. What changes can you make to your prayer life to eliminate one or more of the obstacles discussed in this chapter? Be as specific as possible in your answer.

One from the heart

Based on what you've learned about the different obstacles to passionate prayer, write your own prayer to God. Try to focus on eliminating one or more of the obstacles in your life. And try to be as specific as possible throughout your prayer.

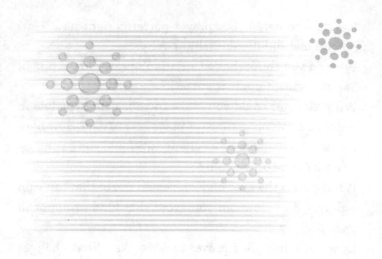

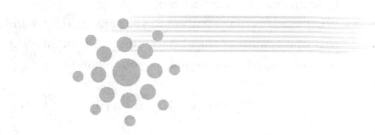

The author gratefully acknowledges . . .

Ann Southern, who made this book possible;

Paige Drygas, who demonstrated patience and persistence
beyond the call of editorial duty;

Friends and family members who prayed
this book to completion;

And Steve and Susie Southern, who taught the importance of
prayer—not with their words, but with their daily habits.

Check out These Other Groovy Products from Extreme for Jesus

Bibles

The Extreme Teen Bible (NKJV)

Hardcover	$24.99	0-7852-0081-9
Paperback	$19.99	0-7852-0082-7
Black Bonded Leather	$39.99	0-7852-5555-9
Deep Purple Bonded Leather	$39.99	0-7852-5525-7
Slimey Limey Green Bonded Leather	$39.99	0-7852-5646-6
Lava Orange Bonded Leather	$39.99	0-7852-5678-4

The Gospel of John	$1.50	0-7852-5537-0

Extreme Word Bible (NKJV)

Paperback	$19.99	0-7852-5732-2
Pitch-Black Bonded Leather	$39.99	0-7852-5735-7
Chromium Hardcover	$29.99	0-7852-5733-0
Blue Snake Hardcover	$29.99	0-7852-5796-9

The Extreme Teen Bible (NCV)

Paperback	$19.99	0-7852-5834-5
Hardcover	$24.99	0-7852-5835-3
Retread Grey	$39.99	0-7180-0063-3
Reigncoat Vinyl	$39.99	0-7180-0062-5

Books

Extreme A-Z: Find it in the Bible	$19.99	0-7852-4580-4
Extreme Answers to Extreme Questions	$12.99	0-7852-4594-4
Extreme Journey: Get More Out of It	$14.99	0-7852-4595-2
The Dictionary: Meaning in God's Words	$19.99	0-7852-4611-8

Burn—Live the Compassion of Jesus	$9.99	0-7852-6746-8
Genuine, by Stacie Orrico (with CD)	$13.99	0-8499-9545-0
Extreme Faith	$10.99	0-7852-6757-3
God's Promises Rock (Your World)	$3.99	0-8499-9507-8
Extreme for Jesus Promise Book	$13.99	0-8499-5606-4

Devotionals
30 Days With Jesus	$7.99	0-7852-6626-5
Extreme Encounters	$9.99	0-7852-5657-1

Workbook
Step Off: Hardest 30 Days	$19.99	0-7852-4604-5

Journals
Xt4J Journal, Plastic Cover	$9.99	0-8499-5710-9
Xt4J Journal, Spiral bound hardcover	$9.99	0-8499-9508-6

Calendar
No Repeat Days	$9.99	0-8499-9510-8

Extreme Faith, a **2001 ECPA Gold Medallion Book Award Winner**, is a collection of fresh, youth-oriented character studies that show readers what a difference young people made in Bible times. This book devotes a chapter to each character profile, telling stories of amazing Bible characters such as Isaac, Esther, and Josiah in detail and showing how today's youth can follow their examples and make a difference in their world. Includes snapshot profiles of modern young people whose lives are extreme for Jesus.

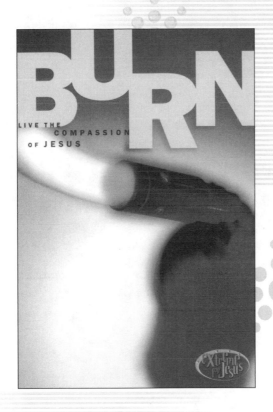

There are people in real need around us every day.
Burn helps Christians express compassion at school,
at home, at work, and anywhere else they go. They learn
about the scriptural mandate for radical compassion—
and are encouraged to become aware of those who are
truly in need: physically, emotionally, or spiritually. *Burn*
is an inspiring guide for those who want to make a real
difference in people's lives.